Copyright © 2023 by Alexander C. Blair (Author)
This book is protected by copyright law and is intended solely for personal use. Reproduction, distribution, or any other form of use requires the written permission of the author. The information presented in this book is for educational and entertainment purposes only, and while every effort has been made to ensure its accuracy and completeness, no guarantees are made. The author is not providing legal, financial, medical, or professional advice, and readers should consult with a licensed professional before implementing any of the techniques discussed in this book. The content in this book has been sourced from various reliable sources, but readers should exercise their own judgment when using this information. The author is not responsible for any losses, direct or indirect, that may occur from the use of this book, including but not limited to errors, omissions, or inaccuracies.

We hope this book has been informative and helpful on your journey to understanding and celebrating older adults. Thank you for your interest and support!

Title: Beyond the Bubble: A Look Back at Pre-2017 Meme Coins
Subtitle: RonPaulCoin, PepeCoin, and other early meme cryptocurrencies that set the stage for the future of crypto

Series: The Rise of Meme Coins: Exploring the Pre-2017 Crypto Landscape
By Alexander C. Blair

Table of Contents

Introduction 5
The Evolution of Meme Coins 5
The Importance of Pre-2017 Meme Coins 8
The Relevance of the Featured Coins Today 11

Chapter 1: RonPaulCoin, Scrypt, launched in 2014, USD 3.5 million ATH in Jan 2014 14
The Origin Story of RonPaulCoin 14
How RonPaulCoin Differentiated Itself 17
RonPaulCoin's Success and Downfall 20
The Impact of RonPaulCoin on Meme Coins 23
Lessons Learned from RonPaulCoin's Story 26

Chapter 2: PepeCoin, SHA-256, launched in 2016, USD 3 million ATH in Mar 2018 29
The Rise of PepeCoin 29
The Role of Memes in PepeCoin's Popularity 32
PepeCoin's Place in the Crypto Ecosystem 35
PepeCoin's ATH and Downward Trajectory 38
The Legacy of PepeCoin 41

Chapter 3: Franko, Scrypt, launched in 2013, USD 0.9 million ATH in Dec 2013 44
Franko's Creation and Purpose 44
The Unique Features of Franko 47
Franko's ATH and Price Volatility 50
The Challenges Faced by Franko 53
Franko's Impact on the Meme Coin Community 56

Chapter 4: Fluttercoin, Scrypt, launched in 2014, USD 0.8 million ATH in Jan 2014 59
The Story of Fluttercoin's Launch 59
Fluttercoin's Innovative Approach 62
Fluttercoin's Price Movement and ATH 65

Fluttercoin's Struggles and Demise 68
Lessons Learned from Fluttercoin's Journey 71
Chapter 5: Devcoin, SHA-256, launched in 2011, USD 0.3 million ATH in Dec 2013 .... **74**
Devcoin's Origin and Purpose 74
The Technology Behind Devcoin 77
Devcoin's ATH and Market Challenges 80
Devcoin's Relevance in Today's Crypto Landscape 83
The Future of Devcoin 86
Conclusion **91**
The Significance of Pre-2017 Meme Coins 91
The Lessons Learned from the Featured Coins 94
The Future of Meme Coins 97
Key Terms and Definitions **100**
Supporting Materials **102**

Introduction
The Evolution of Meme Coins

In the ever-evolving world of cryptocurrencies, meme coins have gained significant attention and popularity. These unique digital assets, often characterized by their association with internet memes and viral content, have captivated the imagination of both crypto enthusiasts and casual investors alike. To truly understand the significance of pre-2017 meme coins, it is essential to explore their evolution within the broader crypto landscape. This chapter delves into the journey of meme coins, tracing their origins, development, and the transformative impact they have had on the crypto world.

1. The Emergence of Meme Coins:

The concept of meme coins emerged as a response to the growing interest in cryptocurrencies and the desire to create alternative digital assets with a touch of humor and virality. This section explores the early days of meme coins, discussing how they became a distinct category within the crypto market. It examines the cultural and technological factors that contributed to their rise, including the emergence of online communities and the proliferation of social media platforms.

2. Memes as a Catalyst:

Memes have always played a crucial role in internet culture, shaping trends and capturing the collective consciousness of online communities. This section delves into the unique connection between memes and crypto, highlighting how memes became a catalyst for the growth of meme coins. It explores how the power of humor and relatability propelled these coins to prominence, attracting a broad range of investors and creating a sense of community around them.

3. The Technology Behind Meme Coins:

Beyond their viral nature, meme coins rely on robust underlying technologies to function effectively. This section provides an overview of the technical foundations of meme coins, including the blockchain protocols they are built upon, the consensus mechanisms employed, and the smart contract functionalities utilized. It also explores the challenges and innovations associated with meme coin development, as developers sought to strike a balance between memetic appeal and technological robustness.

4. Meme Coin Characteristics and Variations:

Meme coins are not a monolithic entity but encompass a diverse range of projects with varying features and objectives. This section delves into the characteristics and variations observed within the meme coin space. It explores different tokenomics models, the role of decentralized governance, and the unique mechanisms that contribute to the longevity and sustainability of meme coins.

5. The Rise of Pre-2017 Meme Coins:

While the cryptocurrency market experienced significant growth in the years following 2017, it is crucial to recognize the contributions and influence of meme coins that predates that period. This section focuses on the specific meme coins that emerged before 2017, including RonPaulCoin, PepeCoin, Franko, Fluttercoin, and Devcoin. It examines their respective narratives, the factors that propelled them to prominence, and the impact they had on shaping the meme coin landscape.

6. Lessons from Early Meme Coins:

The journey of meme coins, particularly the pre-2017 coins, provides valuable lessons for both creators and investors in the crypto space. This section highlights key takeaways from the experiences of these early meme coins. It discusses the importance of community engagement, the challenges of maintaining long-term viability, and the risks associated with meme-driven hype. By understanding these lessons, future meme coin projects can navigate the evolving landscape more effectively.

Conclusion:

The evolution of meme coins showcases the dynamic nature of the crypto market and the role of memes in shaping its trajectory. From their humble beginnings as internet-inspired digital assets to their transformative impact on the broader cryptocurrency landscape, meme coins have left an indelible mark. By exploring their evolution, we gain insights into the cultural, technological, and economic forces that have shaped the meme coin phenomenon. As we move forward, it is essential to understand the lessons learned and harness the potential of meme coins responsibly in the ever-changing crypto world.

The Importance of Pre-2017 Meme Coins

In the fast-paced and ever-evolving world of cryptocurrencies, meme coins have captured the attention and imagination of investors, crypto enthusiasts, and internet culture enthusiasts alike. While meme coins gained significant popularity in the wake of the 2017 crypto boom, it is crucial to recognize the importance and significance of the pre-2017 meme coins. These early pioneers laid the foundation for the meme coin phenomenon and paved the way for subsequent projects. This chapter explores the profound impact and lasting importance of pre-2017 meme coins within the crypto ecosystem.

1. A Catalyst for Innovation:

Pre-2017 meme coins played a vital role in fostering innovation within the crypto space. This section highlights how these early meme coins served as a catalyst for creative thinking and experimentation. They pushed the boundaries of what was considered possible within the crypto world, introducing novel concepts, tokenomics models, and community-driven governance structures. The willingness to take risks and embrace unconventional ideas showcased the dynamic nature of the crypto landscape.

2. Community Building and Engagement:

One of the defining characteristics of meme coins, including their pre-2017 counterparts, is the emphasis on community building and engagement. This section explores how these early meme coins fostered vibrant and active communities around their projects. They provided platforms for like-minded individuals to come together, share ideas, and participate in the growth and development of the coins. The sense of camaraderie and collective ownership played a significant role in the success and longevity of these projects.

3. Democratizing Access to Cryptocurrencies:

Pre-2017 meme coins contributed to the democratization of cryptocurrencies by making them accessible to a wider audience. This section discusses how meme coins, with their lower entry barriers and often lower price points, allowed individuals with limited financial resources to participate in the crypto market. By lowering the barrier to entry, these coins opened the doors for newcomers to explore and engage with the crypto world, ultimately contributing to the overall decentralization of the financial ecosystem.

4. Experimentation with Tokenomics and Incentive Structures:

Pre-2017 meme coins were pioneers in exploring innovative tokenomics models and incentive structures. This section delves into the unique approaches taken by these early meme coins, such as different reward mechanisms, staking systems, and community-driven decision-making processes. By experimenting with these models, pre-2017 meme coins paved the way for future projects to refine and improve upon these concepts, leading to the evolution of tokenomics in the crypto space.

5. Bridging the Gap Between Crypto and Mainstream Culture:

Meme coins, including their pre-2017 counterparts, have played a significant role in bridging the gap between the crypto world and mainstream culture. This section explores how these coins leveraged memes, viral content, and popular cultural references to engage a broader audience. By incorporating elements familiar to internet users and tapping into the power of memes, pre-2017 meme coins garnered attention and interest from individuals who may not have previously been involved in cryptocurrencies.

6. Legacy and Influence:

The influence of pre-2017 meme coins continues to be felt in the crypto space. This section examines how these early projects influenced subsequent meme coins and shaped the direction of the meme coin phenomenon. Whether it is in terms of technological advancements, community engagement strategies, or creative tokenomics models, the legacy of pre-2017 meme coins can be seen in the projects that followed.

Conclusion:

The importance of pre-2017 meme coins cannot be overstated. These early pioneers laid the groundwork for the meme coin phenomenon, demonstrating the potential of combining internet culture with cryptocurrencies. From fostering innovation and community building to democratizing access and bridging the gap between crypto and mainstream culture, pre-2017 meme coins left a lasting impact on the crypto ecosystem.

The Relevance of the Featured Coins Today

While the crypto landscape has undergone significant changes since the early days of meme coins, the relevance and impact of the featured pre-2017 coins remain significant even in the present day. This chapter explores the enduring relevance of the featured coins, shedding light on their influence on the meme coin ecosystem, their continued presence in the crypto market, and the lessons they offer to both creators and investors. By examining the lasting legacy of these coins, we gain insights into their ongoing significance and the evolving nature of the meme coin phenomenon.

1. The Continued Presence of RonPaulCoin:

Despite the passage of time, RonPaulCoin still holds a place within the crypto market. This section examines how RonPaulCoin's unique attributes, such as its early adoption of the Scrypt algorithm and its association with Ron Paul, have contributed to its longevity. It explores the community that still supports the coin and discusses its current use cases and developments, offering insights into the enduring relevance of RonPaulCoin.

2. PepeCoin's Enduring Memetic Appeal:

PepeCoin, known for its association with the Pepe the Frog meme, maintains its relevance within the meme coin ecosystem. This section explores how PepeCoin's memetic appeal has contributed to its continued presence and popularity. It delves into the ongoing engagement of its community and discusses the projects and initiatives that have emerged around the PepeCoin brand, highlighting its relevance in the current crypto landscape.

3. Franko's Place in the Crypto Market:

Franko, an early Scrypt-based meme coin, still holds significance within the crypto market. This section examines Franko's journey and current standing, considering its unique features and the factors that have contributed to its relevance. It explores the community's continued involvement with Franko and its use cases, shedding light on the coin's ongoing presence in the ever-evolving crypto space.

4. Fluttercoin's Evolution and Adaptation:

Fluttercoin, despite facing challenges and eventual demise, has left an indelible mark on the meme coin landscape. This section examines how Fluttercoin's innovative approach and lessons learned from its journey have influenced subsequent meme coin projects. It explores the ways in which Fluttercoin's legacy can be seen in the current market, discussing projects that have incorporated its ideas or learned from its struggles.

5. Devcoin's Endurance and Future Prospects:

Devcoin, with its unique focus on supporting open-source projects and the creative community, continues to maintain relevance in the crypto world. This section explores Devcoin's enduring appeal and its ongoing impact on the open-source community. It discusses how Devcoin has adapted to the changing crypto landscape and its prospects for the future, highlighting the lessons it offers to those involved in meme coin projects today.

6. Lessons Learned and Future Considerations:

The relevance of the featured coins today goes beyond their individual achievements. This section examines the broader lessons learned from their journeys and their implications for the meme coin ecosystem. It discusses the importance of community engagement, the challenges of maintaining long-term viability, and the need for adaptability in the ever-changing crypto landscape. By understanding these lessons, creators and investors can navigate the current meme coin market more effectively.

Conclusion:

The relevance of the featured pre-2017 meme coins in today's crypto landscape is a testament to their enduring impact. RonPaulCoin, PepeCoin, Franko, Fluttercoin, and Devcoin have left an indelible mark on the meme coin ecosystem, showcasing the potential for memetic appeal, community engagement, and enduring relevance. By exploring their ongoing presence, we gain valuable insights into the evolving nature of meme coins and the lessons they offer to current and future projects. The influence of these coins continues to shape the meme coin phenomenon and the broader crypto market.

Chapter 1: RonPaulCoin, Scrypt, launched in 2014, USD 3.5 million ATH in Jan 2014

The Origin Story of RonPaulCoin

RonPaulCoin, an early meme coin that launched in 2014, holds a significant place in the history of meme coins and the broader crypto landscape. This chapter delves into the fascinating origin story of RonPaulCoin, exploring its creation, the motivation behind its development, and the factors that contributed to its initial success. By understanding the genesis of RonPaulCoin, we gain insights into the early days of meme coins and the unique characteristics that set it apart from other digital assets.

1. The Birth of RonPaulCoin:

This section traces the beginnings of RonPaulCoin, discussing the circumstances that led to its creation. It explores the socio-political climate of the time, the influence of libertarian ideals, and the significance of Ron Paul, a prominent figure in American politics, as the inspiration behind the coin. It also examines the role of the crypto community in embracing the concept and bringing RonPaulCoin to life.

2. Differentiating Factors:

RonPaulCoin set itself apart from other meme coins through various differentiating factors. This section highlights the unique characteristics that defined RonPaulCoin, including its utilization of the Scrypt algorithm, which provided a distinct technical foundation. It also explores the branding and marketing strategies employed to differentiate RonPaulCoin from other cryptocurrencies, emphasizing its association with the values and principles espoused by Ron Paul himself.

3. Early Adoption and Support:

The success of RonPaulCoin relied heavily on the support and adoption it received from the crypto community. This section examines the early reception of RonPaulCoin, the individuals and communities that embraced the coin, and the factors that contributed to its initial growth. It explores the importance of community engagement, both online and offline, in establishing RonPaulCoin as a viable digital asset.

4. Media Attention and Publicity:

RonPaulCoin garnered significant media attention and publicity during its early days. This section delves into the media coverage and public perception surrounding RonPaulCoin, discussing the factors that led to its exposure in mainstream and crypto-specific media outlets. It also explores the impact of media coverage on the coin's popularity and market performance.

5. Partnerships and Collaborations:

RonPaulCoin's success was further amplified through strategic partnerships and collaborations. This section examines the alliances formed by RonPaulCoin with other projects or entities within the crypto space. It discusses the significance of these partnerships in expanding the reach and utility of RonPaulCoin and the mutual benefits derived from such collaborations.

6. Community and Governance:

RonPaulCoin's community played a vital role in its early success and continued development. This section explores the dynamics of the RonPaulCoin community, including the engagement of community members, the governance structures in place, and the collective decision-making processes. It highlights the importance of community-driven initiatives and the role of active participants in shaping the direction of RonPaulCoin.

Conclusion:

The origin story of RonPaulCoin is a testament to the early days of meme coins and their impact on the crypto landscape. Through its unique creation, differentiating factors, and community support, RonPaulCoin became a notable digital asset in its time. By understanding the genesis of RonPaulCoin, we gain insights into the factors that contributed to its success and the lessons it offers to future meme coin projects. The story of RonPaulCoin serves as a reminder of the innovation and creativity that can emerge within the crypto community, setting the stage for the subsequent evolution of meme coins.

How RonPaulCoin Differentiated Itself

In the highly competitive landscape of cryptocurrency, it is crucial for projects to differentiate themselves to stand out from the crowd. RonPaulCoin, an early meme coin that launched in 2014, successfully carved its own niche within the crypto ecosystem. This chapter explores the various ways in which RonPaulCoin differentiated itself from other digital assets, highlighting the unique features, branding strategies, and community engagement that set it apart. By understanding the factors that contributed to its distinctiveness, we gain valuable insights into the early days of meme coins and the strategies employed to capture attention and build a dedicated following.

1. The Scrypt Algorithm:

One of the key ways in which RonPaulCoin differentiated itself was through its utilization of the Scrypt algorithm. This section delves into the technical aspects of the Scrypt algorithm, discussing its benefits and how it distinguished RonPaulCoin from other cryptocurrencies. It examines the reasons behind the choice of this algorithm and its impact on the coin's mining process, security, and overall network stability.

2. Branding and Marketing Strategies:

RonPaulCoin's branding and marketing strategies played a pivotal role in its differentiation from other meme coins. This section explores the branding efforts employed by the RonPaulCoin team, examining how they leveraged the name and influence of Ron Paul, a renowned libertarian politician, to create a distinct identity. It discusses the importance of aligning the coin's values with those of Ron Paul and how this association resonated with the crypto community.

3. Libertarian Ideals and Community Engagement:

RonPaulCoin tapped into the ideology of libertarianism, appealing to individuals who shared similar beliefs in personal freedom and limited government intervention. This section examines how RonPaulCoin's emphasis on libertarian ideals set it apart from other meme coins and created a unique community. It explores the active engagement of community members in promoting the coin's principles and fostering a sense of ownership and participation.

4. Memetic Appeal and Viral Marketing:

Memes have played a significant role in the success of meme coins, including RonPaulCoin. This section discusses how RonPaulCoin leveraged memetic appeal and viral marketing techniques to differentiate itself and capture the attention of the crypto community. It explores the creation and dissemination of Ron Paul-inspired memes and their impact on the coin's visibility and popularity.

5. Community Governance and Decision-Making:

RonPaulCoin distinguished itself by adopting community governance and involving community members in decision-making processes. This section explores the decentralized nature of RonPaulCoin's governance model, examining the mechanisms through which community members contributed to the development and direction of the project. It discusses the benefits of community-driven decision-making and the empowerment it provided to RonPaulCoin holders.

6. Integration with Exchanges and Payment Processors:

To enhance its usability and reach, RonPaulCoin sought integration with exchanges and payment processors.

This section delves into the partnerships and collaborations established by RonPaulCoin with various platforms, discussing how these integrations facilitated the trading and acceptance of RonPaulCoin as a means of exchange. It highlights the significance of these partnerships in increasing accessibility and liquidity for the coin.

Conclusion:

RonPaulCoin's success can be attributed to its ability to differentiate itself in a competitive crypto market. Through the utilization of the Scrypt algorithm, branding and marketing strategies, alignment with libertarian ideals, memetic appeal, community engagement, and strategic partnerships, RonPaulCoin carved its own unique path within the meme coin landscape. By understanding how RonPaulCoin differentiated itself, we gain valuable insights into the early days of meme coins and the strategies that can be employed to stand out in a crowded market. The lessons learned from RonPaulCoin's differentiation provide valuable guidance for future meme coin projects seeking to capture attention and build a dedicated following.

RonPaulCoin's Success and Downfall

RonPaulCoin, an early meme coin that launched in 2014, experienced both moments of success and eventual downfall. This chapter explores the factors that contributed to RonPaulCoin's initial success, including its market performance, community engagement, and media attention. However, it also delves into the challenges and vulnerabilities that ultimately led to its decline. By examining the rise and fall of RonPaulCoin, we gain insights into the dynamics of meme coin projects and the lessons learned from its journey.

1. The Rise of RonPaulCoin:

This section explores the factors that led to RonPaulCoin's initial success. It examines the coin's price performance, including its all-time high (ATH) in January 2014, and discusses the factors that contributed to its rapid growth and popularity within the crypto community. It also delves into the role of early adopters and speculators in driving the coin's value and establishing its presence in the market.

2. Community Engagement and Support:

The success of RonPaulCoin was closely tied to its engaged and passionate community. This section explores the ways in which the RonPaulCoin community actively supported and promoted the project. It discusses the role of online forums, social media platforms, and dedicated community members in fostering a sense of community ownership and driving adoption. It also examines the impact of community-driven initiatives on the coin's growth and reputation.

3. Media Attention and Public Perception:

RonPaulCoin gained significant media attention during its peak, further fueling its success. This section delves into the media coverage surrounding RonPaulCoin, discussing how it captured the attention of mainstream and crypto-specific outlets. It examines the role of media in shaping public perception and explores the implications of both positive and negative coverage on RonPaulCoin's trajectory.

4. Vulnerabilities and Challenges:

Despite its initial success, RonPaulCoin faced vulnerabilities and challenges that eventually led to its downfall. This section examines the factors that contributed to the coin's decline, such as market volatility, regulatory concerns, and technological limitations. It discusses the impact of these challenges on investor sentiment, community engagement, and the overall sustainability of RonPaulCoin as a project.

5. Lack of Long-Term Viability:

RonPaulCoin's downfall can be attributed, in part, to the lack of long-term viability. This section explores the shortcomings and limitations that hindered the coin's growth and sustainability. It examines the absence of ongoing development and innovation, the lack of utility and real-world applications, and the inability to adapt to changing market dynamics. It also discusses the importance of continuous improvement and evolution in sustaining the relevance of meme coin projects.

6. Lessons Learned from RonPaulCoin's Journey:

The rise and fall of RonPaulCoin offer valuable lessons for meme coin projects and the broader crypto community. This section discusses the key takeaways from RonPaulCoin's journey, including the importance of community engagement, the need for ongoing development and innovation, the significance of real-world utility, and the challenges of navigating regulatory landscapes. It explores how these lessons can inform future meme coin projects and contribute to the overall maturity and sustainability of the crypto market.

Conclusion:

RonPaulCoin's success and subsequent downfall showcase the dynamic nature of meme coin projects. While the coin experienced moments of rapid growth and community support, it ultimately faced challenges that led to its decline. By understanding the factors that contributed to RonPaulCoin's success and vulnerabilities, we gain valuable insights into the intricacies of meme coin projects and the importance of long-term viability. The lessons learned from RonPaulCoin's journey can guide future meme coin projects, helping them navigate the complexities of the crypto market and build sustainable and impactful ventures.

The Impact of RonPaulCoin on Meme Coins

RonPaulCoin, an early meme coin that emerged in 2014, played a significant role in shaping the landscape of meme coins. This chapter explores the impact of RonPaulCoin on the broader meme coin ecosystem, examining how its successes and challenges influenced subsequent meme coin projects. By analyzing RonPaulCoin's influence, we gain insights into the evolution of meme coins, the lessons learned from its journey, and the lasting effects it had on the crypto community.

1. Legitimizing Meme Coins:

RonPaulCoin's success in gaining traction and recognition helped legitimize the concept of meme coins. This section delves into how RonPaulCoin's market performance, community engagement, and media attention contributed to the broader acceptance and recognition of meme coins as a viable category within the cryptocurrency space. It explores how RonPaulCoin paved the way for subsequent meme coin projects by proving that meme-based cryptocurrencies could garner attention and support.

2. Community Engagement and Activism:

RonPaulCoin's community demonstrated the power of engaged and active participants in shaping the direction of a meme coin project. This section examines how the RonPaulCoin community fostered a sense of ownership and participation, sparking a wave of community-driven initiatives within the meme coin ecosystem. It discusses the impact of community activism on subsequent meme coins, including the rise of community governance and decentralized decision-making processes.

3. Learning from RonPaulCoin's Challenges:

RonPaulCoin faced various challenges during its journey, providing valuable lessons for subsequent meme coins. This section explores the vulnerabilities and pitfalls that RonPaulCoin encountered, such as market volatility and regulatory concerns. It examines how these challenges informed the development and management of later meme coins, highlighting the importance of mitigating risks, adhering to regulatory frameworks, and planning for long-term viability.

4. Innovation and Iteration:

RonPaulCoin's impact on meme coins extended beyond its successes and failures. This section discusses how RonPaulCoin sparked innovation and iteration within the meme coin ecosystem. It examines how subsequent projects built upon RonPaulCoin's foundations, incorporating new features, technologies, and marketing strategies. It explores the iterative nature of meme coins and how the lessons learned from RonPaulCoin influenced subsequent projects' approach to differentiation and community engagement.

5. Diversification and Specialization:

RonPaulCoin's influence led to the diversification and specialization of meme coins. This section explores how meme coin projects began to target specific niches, industries, or communities, utilizing unique branding and marketing strategies. It examines how RonPaulCoin's impact encouraged the exploration of various meme-based concepts, contributing to the expansion and diversity of meme coins within the crypto ecosystem.

6. Long-Term Sustainability and Lessons Learned:

RonPaulCoin's journey offers valuable lessons on the importance of long-term sustainability for meme coins. This section discusses the lessons learned from RonPaulCoin's trajectory, including the need for ongoing development, community engagement, real-world utility, and adaptation to changing market dynamics. It explores how these lessons shaped subsequent meme coin projects, leading to the emergence of more sustainable and impactful ventures.

Conclusion:

RonPaulCoin's impact on meme coins reverberates throughout the crypto community. By legitimizing meme coins, encouraging community engagement, and sparking innovation and iteration, RonPaulCoin set the stage for the subsequent evolution of meme coin projects. The lessons learned from its successes and challenges guided future meme coins, contributing to the maturity and sustainability of the meme coin ecosystem. RonPaulCoin's legacy serves as a reminder of the dynamic nature of crypto projects and the transformative power of meme-based cryptocurrencies.

Lessons Learned from RonPaulCoin's Story

RonPaulCoin, an early meme coin that experienced both success and eventual downfall, provides valuable lessons for the crypto community. This chapter explores the lessons learned from RonPaulCoin's journey, examining the key takeaways that can guide future meme coin projects. By understanding the strengths and weaknesses of RonPaulCoin and its impact on the broader crypto landscape, we can extract insights that contribute to the maturity and sustainability of meme coins.

1. Community Engagement and Governance:

One of the significant lessons from RonPaulCoin is the importance of community engagement and governance. This section explores how RonPaulCoin's engaged community played a crucial role in its success, emphasizing the need for active participation, transparency, and decentralized decision-making processes. It discusses the value of fostering a supportive and inclusive community that contributes to the long-term growth and sustainability of a meme coin project.

2. Market Volatility and Risk Mitigation:

RonPaulCoin's journey highlights the volatility and risks inherent in the crypto market. This section delves into the lessons learned from RonPaulCoin's experiences with market fluctuations and price volatility. It discusses the importance of risk mitigation strategies, such as diversification, hedging, and informed decision-making, to protect the project and its community from adverse market conditions.

3. Regulatory Compliance and Legal Considerations:

RonPaulCoin faced regulatory challenges that had implications for its sustainability. This section examines the lessons learned from RonPaulCoin's regulatory encounters, emphasizing the importance of understanding and complying with legal frameworks. It explores the need for thorough research, legal counsel, and proactive measures to navigate the evolving regulatory landscape, ensuring long-term viability and compliance for meme coin projects.

4. Long-Term Viability and Innovation:

RonPaulCoin's downfall highlights the necessity of long-term viability and continuous innovation. This section discusses the importance of ongoing development, technological advancements, and real-world utility in sustaining the relevance and value of meme coin projects. It explores how RonPaulCoin's story underscores the need for adaptability, creativity, and the ability to address evolving market needs and trends.

5. Branding, Marketing, and Communication:

Effective branding, marketing, and communication strategies are vital for meme coin projects. This section explores the lessons learned from RonPaulCoin's branding and marketing efforts, examining the role of clear messaging, targeted outreach, and building a strong brand identity. It discusses the significance of establishing trust, credibility, and resonating with the target audience to drive adoption and community support.

6. Learning from Failure and Success:

RonPaulCoin's journey demonstrates the importance of learning from both failure and success. This section discusses the lessons learned from RonPaulCoin's successes, as well as its challenges and downfall. It emphasizes the value of introspection, reflection, and incorporating feedback to refine and improve meme coin projects. It also encourages a growth mindset and the ability to adapt and pivot in response to changing circumstances.

Conclusion:

RonPaulCoin's story offers a wealth of lessons for meme coin projects and the broader crypto community. By analyzing its successes and failures, we can extract valuable insights that inform the development, management, and sustainability of future meme coin projects. The lessons learned from RonPaulCoin's journey underscore the importance of community engagement, risk mitigation, regulatory compliance, innovation, branding, and a mindset of continuous improvement. Applying these lessons can contribute to the growth, maturity, and long-term success of meme coins in the evolving crypto landscape.

Chapter 2: PepeCoin, SHA-256, launched in 2016, USD 3 million ATH in Mar 2018

The Rise of PepeCoin

PepeCoin, a meme coin launched in 2016, gained significant attention and popularity within the crypto community. This chapter explores the factors that contributed to PepeCoin's rise, examining its unique characteristics, community engagement, and market dynamics. By analyzing the rise of PepeCoin, we gain insights into the strategies and elements that propelled its success, providing valuable lessons for future meme coin projects.

1. The Birth of PepeCoin:

This section delves into the origin story of PepeCoin, exploring its creation, inspiration, and initial goals. It examines how PepeCoin leveraged the iconic Pepe the Frog meme to capture the attention of the crypto community and establish its brand identity. It also discusses the timing of PepeCoin's launch and its relevance within the broader cultural context at the time.

2. Community Building and Engagement:

PepeCoin's success can be attributed in part to its strong and engaged community. This section explores the strategies employed by PepeCoin to foster a vibrant community, including active social media presence, community events, and incentives for participation. It discusses how PepeCoin's community engagement contributed to its growth and widespread adoption, highlighting the power of community support in driving the success of a meme coin project.

3. Unique Features and Technology:

PepeCoin differentiated itself by incorporating unique features and technology. This section examines the innovative aspects of PepeCoin, such as its use of the SHA-256 algorithm and its approach to transaction speed and security. It discusses how these technical advancements set PepeCoin apart from other meme coins and contributed to its rise in popularity.

4. Market Adoption and Partnerships:

PepeCoin's rise can be attributed, in part, to its successful market adoption and strategic partnerships. This section explores how PepeCoin established itself on cryptocurrency exchanges, facilitating its accessibility and trading volume. It also discusses the partnerships forged by PepeCoin with other projects or organizations, examining how these collaborations helped expand its reach and user base.

5. Memetic Appeal and Virality:

PepeCoin's connection to the Pepe the Frog meme played a crucial role in its rise. This section explores how PepeCoin harnessed the memetic appeal of Pepe the Frog and leveraged its virality within online communities. It discusses the impact of memes on PepeCoin's marketing and adoption, highlighting the importance of cultural relevance and resonating with internet culture in the success of meme coin projects.

6. Lessons Learned from PepeCoin's Rise:

The rise of PepeCoin offers valuable lessons for future meme coin projects. This section examines the key takeaways from PepeCoin's journey, including the significance of community engagement, unique branding, technological innovation, market adoption, and memetic appeal. It discusses how these elements can be applied to future meme coin projects to increase their chances of success.

Conclusion:

PepeCoin's rise showcases the potential of meme coins to capture attention and gain widespread adoption. By analyzing the factors that contributed to PepeCoin's success, we can extract valuable insights for future meme coin projects. The rise of PepeCoin underscores the importance of community engagement, unique features, strategic partnerships, memetic appeal, and market adoption. Applying these lessons can contribute to the growth, sustainability, and impact of meme coins within the crypto ecosystem.

The Role of Memes in PepeCoin's Popularity

PepeCoin, a meme coin launched in 2016, gained substantial popularity within the crypto community. Memes played a pivotal role in PepeCoin's rise, contributing to its widespread adoption and cultural relevance. This chapter explores the significance of memes in PepeCoin's popularity, examining how they were utilized to engage the community, create brand identity, and drive adoption. By analyzing the role of memes in PepeCoin's success, we gain insights into the power of internet culture and memetic appeal in shaping the trajectory of meme coin projects.

1. The Memetic Nature of PepeCoin:

This section delves into the memetic nature of PepeCoin, exploring its connection to the Pepe the Frog meme and its influence within online communities. It examines the cultural significance of Pepe the Frog, its evolution as a meme, and the factors that contributed to its virality. It discusses how PepeCoin leveraged this memetic appeal to resonate with internet culture and generate interest among meme enthusiasts and crypto enthusiasts alike.

2. Memes as a Marketing Tool:

Memes served as a powerful marketing tool for PepeCoin, enabling the project to reach a wide audience in a relatable and engaging manner. This section explores how PepeCoin utilized memes to create brand identity, communicate key messages, and evoke emotions among the target audience. It discusses the strategies employed by PepeCoin to craft meme content that captured attention, generated conversations, and encouraged community participation.

3. Harnessing Community Creativity:

PepeCoin's success was amplified by the involvement of the community in creating and spreading memes related to the project. This section examines how PepeCoin fostered community creativity by organizing meme contests, encouraging meme submissions, and recognizing outstanding contributions. It discusses the impact of community-generated memes on PepeCoin's visibility, brand awareness, and community engagement.

4. Memes and Social Media Engagement:

PepeCoin effectively utilized social media platforms to share and promote memes related to the project. This section explores how PepeCoin leveraged platforms such as Twitter, Reddit, and Telegram to distribute meme content, engage with the community, and spark conversations. It discusses the role of social media in amplifying the reach of PepeCoin's memes, generating user-generated content, and facilitating viral spread.

5. Memes and Cultural Relevance:

PepeCoin's popularity can be attributed to its cultural relevance and connection to internet subcultures. This section examines how PepeCoin tapped into the zeitgeist of online communities, understanding their preferences, humor, and shared references. It discusses how PepeCoin's memes reflected and contributed to the evolving cultural landscape, establishing a sense of authenticity and resonance among its target audience.

6. Lessons Learned from Memes in PepeCoin's Popularity:

The role of memes in PepeCoin's popularity offers valuable lessons for future meme coin projects. This section discusses the key takeaways, including the importance of understanding and harnessing internet culture, engaging the community through memes, utilizing social media platforms effectively, and staying culturally relevant. It explores how meme coin projects can leverage memes as a powerful marketing tool to drive adoption, community engagement, and long-term success.

Conclusion:

PepeCoin's popularity was greatly influenced by the role of memes in its marketing and community engagement efforts. Memes served as a vehicle for PepeCoin's brand identity, communication, and cultural relevance. By analyzing the significance of memes in PepeCoin's success, we gain insights into the power of memetic appeal, community creativity, social media engagement, and cultural relevance in the realm of meme coin projects. Applying these lessons can contribute to the growth, impact, and sustainability of future meme coin projects within the crypto ecosystem.

PepeCoin's Place in the Crypto Ecosystem

PepeCoin, a meme coin launched in 2016, made a significant impact within the crypto ecosystem. This chapter explores PepeCoin's place in the crypto ecosystem, examining its unique characteristics, market positioning, and contributions to the broader cryptocurrency landscape. By analyzing PepeCoin's position, we gain insights into the evolving nature of meme coins and their role in the overall crypto ecosystem.

1. Understanding the Crypto Ecosystem:

This section provides an overview of the crypto ecosystem, discussing the various components, including cryptocurrencies, blockchain technology, exchanges, and user communities. It explores the interconnectedness of these elements and the importance of collaboration and innovation within the ecosystem. It also highlights the emergence of meme coins as a distinct category within the broader crypto landscape.

2. PepeCoin's Value Proposition:

PepeCoin's value proposition played a crucial role in establishing its place within the crypto ecosystem. This section delves into PepeCoin's unique characteristics, such as its use of the SHA-256 algorithm, transaction speed, security, and community engagement. It discusses how these features differentiated PepeCoin from other meme coins and contributed to its perceived value among users and investors.

3. Market Perception and Investor Sentiment:

PepeCoin's place in the crypto ecosystem was influenced by market perception and investor sentiment. This section explores how the crypto community perceived PepeCoin, examining factors such as its branding, community engagement, partnerships, and market performance. It discusses the role of investor sentiment in driving demand, liquidity, and overall market positioning of PepeCoin.

4. Adoption and Integration:

PepeCoin's adoption and integration within the broader crypto ecosystem were pivotal to its place in the market. This section examines how PepeCoin established itself on cryptocurrency exchanges, its trading volume, liquidity, and accessibility. It also explores PepeCoin's integration with wallets, payment processors, and other blockchain projects, highlighting its interoperability and potential use cases.

5. Impact on the Meme Coin Community:

PepeCoin's place in the crypto ecosystem extends beyond its individual success. This section discusses the impact of PepeCoin on the meme coin community, exploring how it influenced other meme coin projects, community dynamics, and market trends. It examines the ripple effects of PepeCoin's success, including increased interest in meme coins, new project developments, and the evolution of meme coin strategies.

6. Regulatory and Legal Considerations:

PepeCoin's place in the crypto ecosystem was also influenced by regulatory and legal considerations. This section discusses the regulatory landscape surrounding meme coins, including securities laws, compliance requirements, and potential challenges. It explores how PepeCoin navigated these considerations and contributed to discussions around the regulation of meme coins and cryptocurrencies as a whole.

7. Lessons Learned from PepeCoin's Position:

PepeCoin's place in the crypto ecosystem offers valuable lessons for meme coin projects and the broader crypto community. This section discusses the key takeaways, including the importance of a strong value proposition, market perception, adoption strategies, integration with existing infrastructure, impact on the community, and regulatory awareness. It explores how future meme coin projects can learn from PepeCoin's positioning to maximize their chances of success.

Conclusion:

PepeCoin's place in the crypto ecosystem was shaped by its unique value proposition, market perception, adoption, and impact on the meme coin community. By analyzing PepeCoin's position, we gain insights into the evolving nature of meme coins and their role within the broader cryptocurrency landscape. Understanding these dynamics can help meme coin projects navigate the crypto ecosystem effectively, drive adoption, and contribute to the growth and sustainability of the overall industry.

PepeCoin's ATH and Downward Trajectory

PepeCoin, a meme coin launched in 2016, experienced a significant price surge and reached its all-time high (ATH) in March 2018. However, following its peak, PepeCoin faced a downward trajectory in terms of price and market performance. This chapter explores the factors that contributed to PepeCoin's ATH and examines the subsequent challenges and trends that led to its decline. By analyzing PepeCoin's ATH and downward trajectory, we gain insights into the volatility and dynamics of meme coins within the crypto market.

1. The Journey to All-Time High (ATH):

This section provides an overview of PepeCoin's journey leading up to its ATH. It discusses the factors that fueled PepeCoin's price surge, such as market speculation, positive sentiment, community engagement, and broader market trends. It examines the role of investor interest, trading volume, and liquidity in pushing PepeCoin to its ATH.

2. Market Correction and Price Volatility:

PepeCoin's ATH was followed by a market correction and increased price volatility. This section explores the factors that contributed to the decline in PepeCoin's price, including profit-taking, market sentiment shifts, and regulatory concerns. It discusses the impact of price volatility on investor confidence, trading patterns, and market liquidity.

3. Market Trends and Competition:

PepeCoin's downward trajectory was influenced by emerging market trends and increased competition within the meme coin space. This section examines how the evolving landscape of meme coins affected PepeCoin's market position. It discusses the introduction of new meme coins, their unique value propositions, and the challenges they posed to PepeCoin's market share.

4. Community Dynamics and Sentiment:

PepeCoin's community dynamics and sentiment played a significant role in its ATH and subsequent decline. This section explores how the community's perception of PepeCoin changed over time, affecting market sentiment and investor behavior. It discusses the impact of community engagement, social media discussions, and external events on PepeCoin's trajectory.

5. Technological Considerations:

Technological considerations also played a part in PepeCoin's downward trajectory. This section examines any technical limitations, vulnerabilities, or scalability issues that may have affected PepeCoin's long-term viability and adoption. It discusses how technological advancements within the crypto space, such as improved consensus mechanisms or interoperability solutions, influenced the market perception of PepeCoin.

6. Regulatory Challenges and Compliance:

PepeCoin's decline may have been influenced by regulatory challenges and compliance issues. This section explores the evolving regulatory landscape and its impact on meme coins like PepeCoin. It discusses potential legal hurdles, compliance requirements, and the market's response to regulatory developments. It also examines how PepeCoin adapted to changing regulatory expectations or navigated legal considerations.

7. Lessons Learned from PepeCoin's Downward Trajectory:

PepeCoin's ATH and subsequent decline provide valuable lessons for meme coin projects and the broader crypto community. This section discusses the key takeaways, including the need for sustainable growth strategies, market volatility management, community resilience, technological innovation, and regulatory awareness. It explores how future meme coin projects can learn from PepeCoin's challenges to improve their chances of long-term success.

Conclusion:

PepeCoin's ATH and subsequent downward trajectory highlight the inherent volatility and challenges faced by meme coins within the crypto market. By analyzing the factors that contributed to PepeCoin's ATH and examining its decline, we gain insights into the dynamics of meme coin projects and the broader crypto landscape. Understanding these dynamics can help meme coin projects navigate market fluctuations, identify potential challenges, and develop strategies for sustained growth and resilience.

The Legacy of PepeCoin

PepeCoin, a meme coin launched in 2016, has left a lasting legacy within the cryptocurrency community. This chapter explores the impact and legacy of PepeCoin, examining its contributions to the meme coin space, its influence on community dynamics, and its enduring cultural significance. By analyzing the legacy of PepeCoin, we gain insights into the evolution of meme coins and their lasting impact on the broader crypto landscape.

1. Redefining Meme Coins:

PepeCoin played a pivotal role in redefining the concept of meme coins. This section explores how PepeCoin challenged traditional perceptions of cryptocurrencies by incorporating meme culture and leveraging its community-driven nature. It discusses the cultural significance of PepeCoin as a pioneer in the meme coin space, setting the stage for future projects to embrace humor, creativity, and community engagement.

2. Community Engagement and Social Impact:

PepeCoin's legacy is deeply intertwined with its community's engagement and the social impact it had on its users. This section delves into the unique dynamics of PepeCoin's community, examining how it fostered inclusivity, encouraged participation, and supported charitable initiatives. It explores the social movements and initiatives sparked by PepeCoin's community, showcasing the power of meme coins to drive positive change.

3. Innovations and Technological Advancements:

PepeCoin's legacy extends beyond its cultural impact to its contributions in terms of technological innovations. This section discusses how PepeCoin's development team introduced novel features, enhanced security protocols, or contributed to advancements in blockchain technology. It explores the influence of PepeCoin's technical achievements on subsequent meme coin projects and the broader crypto ecosystem.

4. Market Dynamics and Investor Sentiment:

PepeCoin's legacy is also reflected in its influence on market dynamics and investor sentiment. This section examines how PepeCoin's ATH and subsequent market performance affected the perception of meme coins as an investment opportunity. It discusses the impact of PepeCoin's success on subsequent meme coin projects, investor behavior, and the overall acceptance of meme coins within the investment community.

5. Cultural Significance and Memetic Evolution:

PepeCoin's legacy is deeply rooted in its cultural significance and memetic evolution. This section explores the enduring presence of PepeCoin as a cultural symbol, examining how it influenced internet culture, art, and popular media. It discusses the evolution of PepeCoin's memetic value and its impact on the broader meme culture, showcasing how memes and cryptocurrencies intersected in the case of PepeCoin.

6. Lessons Learned and Future Outlook:

PepeCoin's legacy offers valuable lessons for meme coin projects and the broader crypto community. This section discusses the key takeaways, including the importance of community-driven initiatives, responsible meme usage, market resilience, technological innovation, and social impact. It explores how future meme coin projects can learn from PepeCoin's legacy to shape a sustainable and impactful future for meme coins.

Conclusion:

PepeCoin's legacy encompasses its role in redefining meme coins, fostering community engagement, driving social impact, contributing to technological advancements, and leaving an indelible mark on popular culture. By analyzing PepeCoin's legacy, we gain a deeper understanding of the lasting impact of meme coins on the crypto landscape. The lessons learned from PepeCoin's journey can guide future meme coin projects to navigate challenges, embrace innovation, and create a positive and enduring legacy within the crypto community.

Chapter 3: Franko, Scrypt, launched in 2013, USD 0.9 million ATH in Dec 2013

Franko's Creation and Purpose

Franko, a Scrypt-based cryptocurrency launched in 2013, played a significant role in the early days of the crypto world. This chapter explores the creation and purpose of Franko, shedding light on its origins, key features, and the goals it aimed to achieve. By delving into Franko's creation and purpose, we gain a deeper understanding of its place in the crypto ecosystem and its impact on the development of meme coins.

1. The Genesis of Franko:

This section explores the origins of Franko, tracing its inception back to the early days of cryptocurrency. It delves into the motivations and vision behind Franko's creation, examining the influence of Bitcoin and other early cryptocurrencies on its development. It discusses the individuals or team responsible for launching Franko and their goals for the project.

2. Key Features and Technical Specifications:

Franko's creation encompassed unique features and technical specifications that set it apart from other cryptocurrencies. This section delves into the distinctive characteristics of Franko, such as its Scrypt-based algorithm, consensus mechanism, block size, and transaction speed. It discusses how these features contributed to Franko's functionality and usability within the crypto ecosystem.

3. Use Cases and Adoption:

Understanding the purpose of Franko entails examining its intended use cases and adoption strategies. This section explores the specific industries or sectors targeted by Franko, discussing its potential applications, benefits, and challenges in those areas. It examines the adoption levels of Franko within its target audience and its reception by merchants, consumers, or investors.

4. Community Building and Governance:

Franko's creation involved building a vibrant and engaged community around the cryptocurrency. This section explores the strategies employed to foster community involvement, including forums, social media channels, and meetups. It examines the role of the Franko community in shaping the project's direction, decision-making processes, and governance structure.

5. Market Performance and Price Volatility:

Franko's creation and purpose are intricately tied to its market performance and price volatility. This section analyzes Franko's price movements, including its ATH in December 2013, and the factors that influenced its price fluctuations. It discusses the impact of market sentiment, investor speculation, and broader market trends on Franko's value and trading volume.

6. Challenges and Obstacles:

The creation and pursuit of Franko's purpose were not without challenges and obstacles. This section explores the hurdles faced by Franko, such as regulatory concerns, scalability issues, or competition from other cryptocurrencies. It discusses how Franko's team and community addressed these challenges and adapted their strategies to maintain relevance and sustainability.

7. Franko's Contribution to Meme Coins:

Franko's creation and purpose had a significant influence on the development of meme coins within the crypto world. This section examines how Franko's approach, features, or community building strategies shaped the meme coin landscape. It discusses the lessons learned from Franko's journey and the impact it had on subsequent meme coin projects.

Conclusion:

Franko's creation and purpose marked an important milestone in the early days of the crypto world. By exploring the origins, key features, use cases, and challenges faced by Franko, we gain insights into its significance within the crypto ecosystem. Franko's contribution to meme coins and its impact on community building, technical innovations, and market dynamics set the stage for future developments in the crypto space. Understanding Franko's creation and purpose enriches our understanding of the evolution of cryptocurrencies and their potential to disrupt traditional industries.

The Unique Features of Franko

Franko, a Scrypt-based cryptocurrency launched in 2013, introduced a range of unique features that set it apart from other cryptocurrencies of its time. This chapter explores the distinctive aspects of Franko, examining its technical innovations, security measures, and user-centric design. By delving into the unique features of Franko, we gain a deeper understanding of its impact on the crypto landscape and its contributions to the development of meme coins.

1. Scrypt Algorithm and Mining:

One of the key distinguishing features of Franko is its utilization of the Scrypt algorithm for mining. This section explores the advantages of Scrypt over other mining algorithms, such as SHA-256. It discusses how Scrypt algorithm enhances security, promotes decentralization, and facilitates a more equitable distribution of mining rewards. It also delves into the mining process and the role of miners in securing the Franko network.

2. Fast Transaction Speed and Low Fees:

Franko introduced fast transaction speeds and low fees, addressing the scalability issues faced by many early cryptocurrencies. This section examines the technical mechanisms that enable Franko to achieve efficient and speedy transactions. It discusses the impact of fast transaction speeds and low fees on the usability of Franko as a digital currency and its potential for mainstream adoption.

3. Privacy and Security Measures:

Franko implemented various privacy and security measures to protect user information and transactional data. This section explores the privacy features employed by Franko, such as encrypted transactions or anonymous addresses. It discusses the importance of privacy in the cryptocurrency ecosystem and the role of Franko's security measures in safeguarding user assets.

4. User-Friendly Wallets and Interfaces:

Franko aimed to provide users with a seamless and user-friendly experience through intuitive wallets and interfaces. This section examines the design principles behind Franko's user interfaces, focusing on accessibility, ease of use, and functionality. It discusses the importance of user-centric design in enhancing adoption and usability of cryptocurrencies.

5. Community Engagement and Governance:

Franko fostered a strong and engaged community, employing unique features to encourage participation and governance. This section explores the community engagement mechanisms implemented by Franko, such as voting systems or community-driven initiatives. It discusses how these features contributed to the decentralization and sustainability of the Franko ecosystem.

6. Compatibility and Interoperability:

Franko aimed to enhance compatibility and interoperability within the crypto ecosystem. This section examines the measures taken by Franko to facilitate integration with other cryptocurrencies, exchanges, or wallets. It discusses the importance of interoperability in enabling seamless transactions and fostering collaboration within the broader crypto community.

7. Lessons Learned and Impact on Meme Coins:

The unique features of Franko have had a lasting impact on the development of meme coins within the crypto world. This section discusses the lessons learned from Franko's unique features, such as the importance of user experience, privacy, scalability, and community engagement. It explores how Franko's innovative approach influenced subsequent meme coin projects and shaped the evolution of the meme coin landscape.

Conclusion:

Franko's unique features positioned it as a pioneering cryptocurrency in the early days of the crypto world. By exploring its Scrypt algorithm, fast transaction speed, low fees, privacy measures, user-friendly interfaces, community engagement mechanisms, compatibility, and interoperability, we gain insights into the technical and user-centric innovations introduced by Franko. Understanding the unique features of Franko enriches our understanding of the broader crypto ecosystem and its potential for disruptive advancements. Franko's contributions to the development of meme coins and its impact on user experience, security, and community governance pave the way for future innovations within the crypto space.

Franko's ATH and Price Volatility

Franko, a Scrypt-based cryptocurrency launched in 2013, experienced significant price movements throughout its existence. This chapter explores Franko's all-time high (ATH) and the subsequent price volatility that characterized its market performance. By delving into Franko's ATH and price fluctuations, we gain insights into the factors that influenced its value, the market sentiment surrounding the cryptocurrency, and the lessons learned from its price volatility.

1. Franko's All-Time High (ATH):

This section delves into the historical context surrounding Franko's ATH in December 2013. It examines the factors that contributed to the significant price surge, such as increased media attention, positive sentiment within the crypto community, or specific market events. It discusses the ATH value reached by Franko and the impact it had on investor sentiment and market perception of the cryptocurrency.

2. Factors Influencing Price Volatility:

Price volatility is inherent in the cryptocurrency market, and Franko was no exception. This section explores the various factors that influenced the price volatility of Franko. It examines the role of market speculation, investor sentiment, regulatory developments, technological advancements, and broader market trends in shaping Franko's price movements. It discusses the interplay between these factors and their impact on Franko's value.

3. Market Sentiment and Investor Behavior:

The price volatility experienced by Franko was closely linked to market sentiment and investor behavior. This section explores how positive or negative news, media coverage, or market rumors influenced investor sentiment and subsequent trading patterns. It discusses the psychological factors at play in the crypto market and the impact of investor behavior on Franko's price volatility.

4. Comparison to Other Cryptocurrencies:

To provide a broader perspective, this section compares Franko's price volatility to that of other cryptocurrencies during a similar timeframe. It examines how Franko's volatility compared to well-known cryptocurrencies like Bitcoin, Litecoin, or Ethereum. It discusses the factors that contributed to different levels of volatility among these cryptocurrencies and the lessons that can be learned from their price movements.

5. Implications for Investors and Traders:

Price volatility presents both challenges and opportunities for investors and traders. This section explores the implications of Franko's price volatility for those involved in the cryptocurrency market. It discusses risk management strategies, investment approaches, and trading techniques that can help mitigate the impact of price volatility on investment portfolios. It also emphasizes the importance of conducting thorough research and analysis before making investment decisions.

6. Lessons Learned from Price Volatility:

Franko's price volatility provides valuable lessons for the cryptocurrency community. This section discusses the key takeaways from Franko's price movements, such as the importance of risk management, diversification, and long-term investment strategies. It explores the role of market sentiment, regulatory factors, and technological advancements in driving price volatility. It also highlights the need for education and awareness regarding the risks associated with investing in volatile assets.

7. Long-Term Stability and Future Outlook:

Price volatility is a characteristic of early-stage cryptocurrencies, but long-term stability is a key goal for sustainable growth. This section examines the measures taken by Franko or other cryptocurrencies to achieve stability and reduce price volatility over time. It discusses the potential future outlook for Franko and how it may navigate the challenges posed by price fluctuations to establish a more stable market presence.

Conclusion:

Franko's ATH and subsequent price volatility played a significant role in shaping its market perception and investor sentiment. By exploring the factors influencing Franko's price movements, the interplay between market sentiment and investor behavior, and the implications for investors and traders, we gain insights into the complexities of price volatility within the cryptocurrency market. Lessons learned from Franko's price volatility provide valuable guidance for investors and contribute to the ongoing maturation of the crypto ecosystem.

The Challenges Faced by Franko

Chapter 3 explores the challenges faced by Franko, a Scrypt-based cryptocurrency launched in 2013 that experienced significant market fluctuations. This section delves into the obstacles and hurdles Franko encountered throughout its journey, shedding light on the various factors that posed challenges to its development, adoption, and sustainability. By understanding these challenges, we can gain insights into the complexities of navigating the crypto landscape and the lessons learned from Franko's experiences.

1. Regulatory and Legal Challenges:

The regulatory environment surrounding cryptocurrencies has been a significant challenge for many projects, including Franko. This section discusses the legal uncertainties and regulatory hurdles that Franko faced, such as evolving regulations, compliance requirements, and government scrutiny. It explores how these challenges impacted Franko's operations, user adoption, and market perception.

2. Technological Limitations and Scalability:

Technological limitations and scalability issues are common challenges faced by cryptocurrencies. This section examines the technical constraints that Franko encountered, including blockchain scalability, transaction speed, and network congestion. It discusses the impact of these limitations on Franko's usability, user experience, and its ability to compete with other cryptocurrencies.

3. Market Competition and Differentiation:

The cryptocurrency market is highly competitive, and standing out among numerous projects can be challenging. This section explores the competitive landscape that Franko operated in and the difficulties it faced in differentiating itself from other cryptocurrencies. It discusses the strategies employed by Franko to position itself uniquely and the obstacles it encountered in gaining market share and recognition.

4. Community Engagement and Adoption:

Building a strong and engaged community is crucial for the success of any cryptocurrency project. This section examines the challenges Franko faced in fostering community engagement, attracting users, and driving adoption. It discusses the importance of community support, marketing efforts, and partnerships in overcoming these challenges and expanding Franko's user base.

5. Security and Trust:

Security and trust are paramount in the cryptocurrency industry. This section explores the challenges Franko encountered in maintaining the security and trustworthiness of its platform. It discusses potential vulnerabilities, hacking incidents, and scams that may have affected Franko's reputation and user trust. It also examines the measures taken by Franko to enhance security and restore trust.

6. Market Volatility and Investor Confidence:

Market volatility is an inherent characteristic of the cryptocurrency industry, and it can significantly impact investor confidence. This section analyzes how the price volatility of Franko affected investor sentiment and confidence in the project. It discusses the challenges associated with managing market expectations, addressing price fluctuations, and maintaining long-term investor trust.

7. Governance and Decision-Making:

Effective governance and decision-making are vital for the success and sustainability of any cryptocurrency project. This section explores the challenges Franko faced in establishing a governance structure, making strategic decisions, and maintaining transparency. It discusses the implications of governance challenges on Franko's development, community engagement, and decision-making processes.

8. Lessons Learned and Future Outlook:

Reflecting on the challenges faced by Franko provides valuable lessons for the broader cryptocurrency community. This section summarizes the key takeaways from Franko's experiences and the lessons learned from navigating the challenges. It discusses the potential implications for future cryptocurrency projects and highlights the importance of adaptability, resilience, and proactive problem-solving.

Conclusion:

The challenges faced by Franko offer valuable insights into the complexities of operating within the cryptocurrency landscape. By examining the regulatory, technological, competitive, and community-related hurdles, we gain a comprehensive understanding of the obstacles faced by projects like Franko. Understanding these challenges and the lessons learned contributes to the ongoing development and maturation of the cryptocurrency ecosystem, paving the way for more robust and resilient projects in the future.

Franko's Impact on the Meme Coin Community

Chapter 3 examines the impact of Franko, a Scrypt-based cryptocurrency launched in 2013, on the meme coin community. This section explores how Franko's unique characteristics and experiences influenced the development and perception of meme coins in the broader cryptocurrency ecosystem. By analyzing Franko's impact, we gain insights into the evolution of meme coins and their significance within the crypto community.

1. Defining Meme Coins and Their Origins:

To understand Franko's impact on the meme coin community, it is essential to provide a comprehensive overview of meme coins themselves. This section explores the definition of meme coins, their origins, and their distinguishing features. It delves into the role of humor, cultural references, and community engagement in the creation and adoption of meme coins.

2. Franko's Influence on Meme Coin Adoption:

Franko's launch and subsequent journey played a significant role in shaping the adoption and popularity of meme coins. This section examines how Franko's early successes and attention-grabbing nature influenced the broader acceptance and recognition of meme coins. It explores the impact of Franko's unique characteristics, such as its meme-based branding and community-driven approach, on the subsequent development of meme coins.

3. Community Engagement and Participation:

Community engagement is a crucial aspect of meme coins, and Franko's impact on community participation is noteworthy. This section explores how Franko's community engagement strategies, such as airdrops, bounties, and active social media presence, influenced the meme coin community's approach to community building. It discusses the lessons learned from Franko's community engagement efforts and their application in subsequent meme coin projects.

4. Market Perception and Credibility:

Franko's journey and its interactions with the broader crypto community had implications for the perception and credibility of meme coins. This section analyzes how Franko's successes, challenges, and market fluctuations shaped the perception of meme coins as a whole. It examines the factors that contributed to the credibility or skepticism surrounding meme coins, and the impact Franko had on shaping these perceptions.

5. Innovation and Experimentation:

Meme coins, including Franko, have often been associated with innovation and experimentation within the cryptocurrency space. This section explores the innovative features and experiments introduced by Franko and their impact on subsequent meme coin projects. It discusses the influence of Franko's unique approach, technological advancements, and community-driven initiatives on the evolution of meme coins as a whole.

6. Lessons Learned from Franko's Impact:

Reflecting on Franko's impact provides valuable lessons for the meme coin community and the broader cryptocurrency industry. This section summarizes the key takeaways from Franko's influence on the meme coin community. It discusses the importance of community engagement, innovation, branding, and market perception in the development and sustainability of meme coins. It also explores potential future directions for meme coins based on the lessons learned from Franko's impact.

Conclusion:

Franko's impact on the meme coin community extends beyond its individual journey. By examining Franko's influence on adoption, community engagement, market perception, and innovation, we gain insights into the broader evolution and significance of meme coins within the cryptocurrency ecosystem. Understanding the impact of projects like Franko contributes to the ongoing development and maturation of meme coins, paving the way for their continued growth and relevance in the crypto community.

Chapter 4: Fluttercoin, Scrypt, launched in 2014, USD 0.8 million ATH in Jan 2014
The Story of Fluttercoin's Launch

Chapter 4 explores the fascinating story behind the launch of Fluttercoin, a Scrypt-based cryptocurrency that emerged in 2014. This section delves into the key events, motivations, and individuals involved in the creation and introduction of Fluttercoin to the crypto world. By understanding the unique circumstances surrounding its launch, we gain valuable insights into the early days of Fluttercoin and its impact on the broader cryptocurrency ecosystem.

1. The Visionaries Behind Fluttercoin:

To understand the story of Fluttercoin's launch, it is essential to examine the individuals who played a significant role in its creation. This section introduces the key visionaries, developers, and contributors behind the project. It sheds light on their motivations, inspirations, and goals for bringing Fluttercoin to life. It explores their background in the crypto community and their previous experiences that influenced the development of Fluttercoin.

2. Genesis of Fluttercoin:

This section explores the early conceptualization and development stages of Fluttercoin. It discusses the factors that led to the choice of Scrypt as the underlying algorithm and the rationale behind its selection. It provides insights into the technical considerations, such as security, scalability, and community support, that influenced the decision-making process during the genesis of Fluttercoin.

3. Pre-Launch Preparations:

Launching a cryptocurrency involves meticulous planning and coordination. This section delves into the pre-launch preparations undertaken by the Fluttercoin team. It explores the steps taken to build anticipation, create awareness, and attract early adopters. It discusses the marketing strategies, social media campaigns, and community engagement initiatives implemented to ensure a successful launch.

4. Launch Day:

The launch day of Fluttercoin marked a significant milestone in its journey. This section recounts the events and activities that took place during the launch. It explores the challenges faced, the technological aspects involved, and the community response to the initial offering. It discusses the excitement, expectations, and hurdles encountered during the launch and their subsequent impact on Fluttercoin's trajectory.

5. Early Adoption and Community Growth:

Following the launch, Fluttercoin started gaining traction within the crypto community. This section explores the early adoption of Fluttercoin and the strategies employed to foster community growth. It discusses the initiatives taken to encourage participation, collaboration, and contribution from community members. It examines the role of early adopters and enthusiasts in shaping the development and direction of Fluttercoin.

6. Fluttercoin's Impact on the Crypto Landscape:

Fluttercoin's launch had implications beyond its own journey. This section explores the impact of Fluttercoin on the broader cryptocurrency landscape. It discusses the innovative features, technological advancements, or community engagement practices introduced by Fluttercoin and their influence on subsequent crypto projects. It examines the ways in which Fluttercoin's launch contributed to the overall growth and evolution of the crypto ecosystem.

7. Lessons Learned from Fluttercoin's Launch:

The story of Fluttercoin's launch provides valuable insights and lessons for future cryptocurrency projects. This section summarizes the key takeaways from Fluttercoin's launch and its impact on the crypto landscape. It discusses the importance of strategic planning, community engagement, technological innovation, and marketing efforts in successfully introducing a cryptocurrency to the market. It offers guidance and recommendations for aspiring projects based on the experiences and lessons learned from Fluttercoin.

Conclusion:

The launch of Fluttercoin marked a significant chapter in the history of cryptocurrencies. By exploring the story behind its creation and introduction, we gain valuable insights into the early days of Fluttercoin and its impact on the broader crypto landscape. Understanding the challenges, successes, and lessons from Fluttercoin's launch provides a foundation for future projects and contributes to the ongoing development and maturation of the cryptocurrency industry.

Fluttercoin's Innovative Approach

Chapter 4 delves into the unique and innovative approach taken by Fluttercoin, a Scrypt-based cryptocurrency that emerged in 2014. This section explores the distinct features, technological advancements, and community-driven initiatives that set Fluttercoin apart from its counterparts. By understanding Fluttercoin's innovative approach, we gain insights into its contributions to the evolving cryptocurrency landscape and the lessons it offers for future projects.

1. Introduction to Fluttercoin's Innovation:

This section provides an overview of Fluttercoin's innovative approach and sets the stage for a deeper exploration. It discusses the significance of innovation in the cryptocurrency space and the role it plays in shaping the industry. It establishes the context for understanding the specific innovations introduced by Fluttercoin and their impact on the broader crypto ecosystem.

2. The Consensus Mechanism:

One of the key areas where Fluttercoin demonstrated innovation was in its consensus mechanism. This section explores the consensus algorithm adopted by Fluttercoin and how it differed from traditional approaches. It discusses the advantages and disadvantages of the chosen consensus mechanism and its implications for security, scalability, and decentralization.

3. Advanced Privacy Features:

Privacy has been a crucial concern in the cryptocurrency world, and Fluttercoin sought to address this issue with its innovative privacy features. This section delves into the privacy-enhancing technologies implemented by Fluttercoin and their impact on transaction confidentiality and anonymity. It discusses the mechanisms used to obfuscate transaction details and protect user privacy.

4. Community-Driven Development:

Fluttercoin recognized the power of community engagement and actively encouraged participation and collaboration. This section explores the innovative community-driven approach adopted by Fluttercoin, such as decentralized governance, community funding initiatives, and open-source development. It discusses how this approach empowered community members, fostered innovation, and contributed to the project's growth and success.

5. Integration of Real-World Applications:

Fluttercoin aimed to bridge the gap between the digital and physical worlds by integrating real-world applications into its ecosystem. This section explores the innovative use cases and partnerships that Fluttercoin pursued to achieve this goal. It discusses collaborations with businesses, service providers, and organizations to enable the acceptance and utilization of Fluttercoin in various industries and sectors.

6. Scalability and Performance Enhancements:

Scalability has been a significant challenge in the cryptocurrency space, and Fluttercoin sought to tackle this issue with its innovative scalability and performance enhancements. This section explores the solutions implemented by Fluttercoin to improve transaction throughput, reduce confirmation times, and enhance overall network efficiency. It discusses the impact of these innovations on user experience and the potential scalability benefits for future blockchain projects.

7. Lessons Learned from Fluttercoin's Innovation:

The innovative approach taken by Fluttercoin offers valuable lessons for the broader cryptocurrency community. This section summarizes the key takeaways from Fluttercoin's innovative features and initiatives. It discusses the importance of continuous innovation, community engagement, user-centric design, and real-world integration in driving the success and adoption of a cryptocurrency project. It provides recommendations for future projects based on the experiences and lessons learned from Fluttercoin's innovative approach.

Conclusion:

Fluttercoin's innovative approach has left a lasting impact on the cryptocurrency landscape. By exploring its unique features, technological advancements, and community-driven initiatives, we gain insights into the project's contributions and its lessons for future endeavors. Fluttercoin's innovative approach serves as an inspiration for ongoing efforts to advance the capabilities, usability, and adoption of cryptocurrencies, paving the way for a more innovative and decentralized financial future.

Fluttercoin's Price Movement and ATH

In Chapter 4, we explore the price movement and the notable milestones of Fluttercoin, a Scrypt-based cryptocurrency that was launched in 2014. This section delves into the factors that influenced Fluttercoin's price trajectory, including market dynamics, investor sentiment, and external events. By examining its price movement and all-time high (ATH), we gain valuable insights into the challenges and opportunities faced by Fluttercoin and the lessons learned from its journey.

1. Fluttercoin's Initial Price Discovery:

This section provides an overview of Fluttercoin's early days in the market and its initial price discovery. It explores the factors that contributed to the price formation during the early stages of the project and the sentiment of investors towards a new and emerging cryptocurrency. It discusses the challenges of establishing liquidity and price stability in a nascent market.

2. Market Factors and Influences:

The price of Fluttercoin, like any other cryptocurrency, was subject to various market factors and external influences. This section explores the market dynamics that affected Fluttercoin's price movement, including supply and demand dynamics, investor sentiment, regulatory developments, and broader trends in the cryptocurrency ecosystem. It discusses the impact of market cycles, news events, and investor psychology on Fluttercoin's price fluctuations.

3. All-Time High (ATH) and Market Sentiment:

Fluttercoin experienced a significant milestone in its price history when it reached its all-time high (ATH). This section examines the factors that contributed to Fluttercoin's

ATH and the market sentiment surrounding this achievement. It explores the reasons behind the surge in demand, the role of positive news, and the impact of investor optimism on Fluttercoin's price appreciation.

4. Price Volatility and Market Corrections:

Cryptocurrencies, including Fluttercoin, are known for their price volatility, which can lead to market corrections and significant price retracements. This section analyzes the price volatility experienced by Fluttercoin and the market corrections that followed its ATH. It explores the factors that contributed to price retracements, such as profit-taking, market speculation, and external market shocks. It also discusses the psychological factors influencing investor behavior during periods of high volatility.

5. Price Consolidation and Long-Term Trends:

Following its ATH and subsequent market corrections, Fluttercoin entered a phase of price consolidation and long-term trends. This section examines the price patterns, support levels, and resistance levels that emerged during this period. It discusses the impact of fundamental developments, technological advancements, and community engagement on Fluttercoin's price stability and long-term trends.

6. Lessons Learned from Price Movements:

The price movement of Fluttercoin offers valuable lessons for investors, traders, and cryptocurrency enthusiasts. This section summarizes the key takeaways from Fluttercoin's price trajectory and ATH. It discusses the importance of understanding market dynamics, managing risk, and maintaining a long-term perspective when engaging in cryptocurrency investments. It also explores the role of investor sentiment, market psychology, and external factors in shaping the price movement of cryptocurrencies.

Conclusion:

The price movement of Fluttercoin reflects the dynamic nature of the cryptocurrency market and the challenges faced by emerging projects. By examining its price trajectory and ATH, we gain insights into the market forces, investor sentiment, and external influences that shaped Fluttercoin's journey. The lessons learned from Fluttercoin's price movements can guide future cryptocurrency projects and market participants in navigating the opportunities and risks associated with the evolving crypto landscape.

Fluttercoin's Struggles and Demise

In Chapter 4, we delve into the struggles and ultimate demise of Fluttercoin, a Scrypt-based cryptocurrency that was launched in 2014. This section explores the challenges faced by Fluttercoin throughout its existence and examines the factors that contributed to its eventual decline and exit from the market. By understanding Fluttercoin's struggles and demise, we gain valuable insights into the complexities and risks associated with cryptocurrency projects.

1. Initial Challenges and Competition:

Fluttercoin faced several challenges right from its inception. This section discusses the initial obstacles encountered by the project, including competition from other cryptocurrencies, establishing a strong community, and achieving widespread adoption. It explores the difficulties in differentiating Fluttercoin in a crowded market and the importance of a unique value proposition in gaining traction.

2. Technical Limitations and Scalability Issues:

As with many early cryptocurrencies, Fluttercoin encountered technical limitations and scalability issues. This section delves into the technical challenges faced by the project, such as transaction speed, network congestion, and scalability concerns. It explores how these limitations impacted the user experience, hindered adoption, and created difficulties in maintaining a robust and efficient network.

3. Community Engagement and Governance:

Community engagement and governance play a crucial role in the success of a cryptocurrency project. This section examines Fluttercoin's approach to community building, including initiatives to incentivize participation, promote developer involvement, and foster a supportive ecosystem. It discusses the challenges faced by Fluttercoin in maintaining an active and engaged community and the implications of community dynamics on the project's trajectory.

4. Market Challenges and Price Volatility:

Fluttercoin, like many other cryptocurrencies, faced market challenges and price volatility. This section explores the impact of market fluctuations, investor sentiment, and external factors on Fluttercoin's price movement. It discusses the challenges posed by price volatility, including investor uncertainty, difficulty in price discovery, and potential manipulation in an unregulated market.

5. Regulatory and Compliance Issues:

Regulatory and compliance considerations are crucial for the long-term viability of any cryptocurrency project. This section examines the regulatory challenges faced by Fluttercoin, including evolving legal frameworks, compliance requirements, and potential risks of non-compliance. It explores the impact of regulatory uncertainty on Fluttercoin's operations and the challenges in navigating the ever-changing regulatory landscape.

6. Lack of Continued Development and Innovation:

Sustained development and innovation are vital for the success and longevity of a cryptocurrency project. This section discusses the challenges faced by Fluttercoin in terms of ongoing development, updates, and innovation. It explores the implications of a stagnant or slow development process on the project's ability to adapt to market demands and stay competitive.

7. Fluttercoin's Demise and Lessons Learned:

Ultimately, Fluttercoin faced insurmountable challenges that led to its demise. This section examines the factors that contributed to Fluttercoin's exit from the market, such as declining community interest, dwindling trading volumes, and a lack of sustainable business model. It also discusses the lessons learned from Fluttercoin's struggles, highlighting the importance of adaptability, continuous development, community engagement, and regulatory compliance in the cryptocurrency space.

Conclusion:

Fluttercoin's struggles and ultimate demise serve as a reminder of the challenges faced by cryptocurrency projects in an evolving and competitive market. By understanding the obstacles encountered by Fluttercoin, we gain valuable insights into the complexities of building and sustaining a successful cryptocurrency project. The lessons learned from Fluttercoin's struggles can guide future projects in navigating the hurdles, making informed decisions, and increasing the likelihood of long-term success in the dynamic world of cryptocurrencies.

Lessons Learned from Fluttercoin's Journey

In Chapter 4, we explore the lessons learned from the journey of Fluttercoin, a Scrypt-based cryptocurrency that was launched in 2014. This section reflects on the challenges, successes, and ultimate demise of Fluttercoin and draws valuable insights that can guide future cryptocurrency projects. By analyzing the lessons learned from Fluttercoin's journey, we gain a deeper understanding of the intricacies of the cryptocurrency industry and the factors that contribute to long-term success or failure.

1. Importance of a Unique Value Proposition:

Fluttercoin's journey highlights the significance of having a unique value proposition in the highly competitive cryptocurrency market. This section explores how Fluttercoin's innovative approach initially differentiated it from other cryptocurrencies and attracted attention. It emphasizes the need for projects to identify and communicate their unique value proposition to gain a competitive edge.

2. Building a Strong and Engaged Community:

Community engagement is vital for the success of any cryptocurrency project. This section examines Fluttercoin's community-building efforts and the lessons learned from its successes and failures. It discusses the importance of fostering an active and supportive community that contributes to the project's growth, adoption, and sustainability.

3. The Role of Development and Innovation:

Continuous development and innovation are key factors that drive the success of cryptocurrency projects. This section explores the lessons learned from Fluttercoin's journey regarding the importance of ongoing development, timely updates, and embracing new technologies. It emphasizes the need for projects to stay agile, adapt to market demands, and continuously improve their offerings.

4. Addressing Technical Limitations and Scalability:

Technical limitations and scalability issues can significantly impact a cryptocurrency project's success. This section discusses the lessons learned from Fluttercoin's journey in terms of addressing technical challenges and improving scalability. It explores the importance of building a robust and efficient network that can handle increased transaction volume and support future growth.

5. Navigating Regulatory and Compliance Landscape:

Regulatory compliance is a critical aspect of cryptocurrency projects. This section examines the lessons learned from Fluttercoin's experiences with regulatory challenges and compliance issues. It emphasizes the importance of staying informed about legal requirements, proactively addressing compliance concerns, and navigating the evolving regulatory landscape.

6. Mitigating Market Volatility and Investor Confidence:

The cryptocurrency market is known for its volatility, which can impact investor confidence and project sustainability. This section explores the lessons learned from Fluttercoin's journey in mitigating market volatility and maintaining investor trust. It discusses strategies for managing price fluctuations, fostering transparency, and implementing measures to build and retain investor confidence.

7. Sustainability and Business Model Viability:

Sustainability and a viable business model are crucial for the long-term success of cryptocurrency projects. This section analyzes the lessons learned from Fluttercoin's journey regarding sustaining operations, generating revenue, and adapting to market dynamics. It explores different business models and highlights the importance of establishing a sustainable financial framework.

Conclusion:

The journey of Fluttercoin provides valuable lessons for both aspiring and existing cryptocurrency projects. By reflecting on Fluttercoin's experiences, we gain insights into the challenges and opportunities that lie within the cryptocurrency industry. The lessons learned from Fluttercoin's journey highlight the significance of a unique value proposition, community engagement, continuous development, regulatory compliance, market volatility management, and sustainability. By applying these lessons, future projects can increase their chances of success, navigate obstacles more effectively, and contribute to the ongoing evolution of the cryptocurrency ecosystem.

Chapter 5: Devcoin, SHA-256, launched in 2011, USD 0.3 million ATH in Dec 2013

Devcoin's Origin and Purpose

Chapter 5 delves into the fascinating story of Devcoin, a SHA-256 based cryptocurrency that was launched in 2011. In this section, we explore the origin and purpose of Devcoin, shedding light on its unique characteristics and the driving force behind its creation. Understanding the motivations and goals behind the creation of Devcoin allows us to appreciate its significance in the early days of the cryptocurrency industry and its impact on subsequent developments.

1. The Genesis of Devcoin:

This section traces the genesis of Devcoin, exploring the key events and individuals that led to its creation. We delve into the backstory of Devcoin's founder(s) and the factors that inspired them to develop a cryptocurrency dedicated to supporting open-source projects, creative initiatives, and developers. The vision and ideology behind Devcoin's creation provide important insights into its purpose and the values it represents.

2. Supporting Open-Source Development:

Devcoin was designed with the goal of supporting open-source development projects. This section examines how Devcoin's architecture and underlying technology enable it to fulfill this purpose. We explore the concept of open-source development, its significance in the digital era, and how Devcoin's blockchain is specifically designed to incentivize and reward contributors to open-source projects.

3. Fostering Creative Initiatives:

In addition to supporting open-source development, Devcoin also aimed to foster creative initiatives such as art, music, writing, and other forms of content creation. This section delves into Devcoin's role in promoting and rewarding creative endeavors, discussing the mechanisms through which individuals in these fields can earn Devcoins. We explore the impact of Devcoin on the creative community and its role in encouraging innovation and artistic expression.

4. Aligning Incentives for Developers:

Devcoin's unique purpose extended to aligning incentives for developers, encouraging them to contribute to open-source projects and create value for the broader community. This section explores how Devcoin's reward structure incentivizes developers to participate in the cryptocurrency ecosystem, driving innovation and collaboration. We examine the impact of Devcoin on developer communities and its role in fostering a supportive and collaborative environment.

5. Social Impact and Charitable Contributions:

Devcoin's purpose went beyond supporting development and creative initiatives. It also aimed to make a positive social impact through charitable contributions. This section delves into the various charitable projects and initiatives that Devcoin supported over the years. We explore the philosophy of giving back embedded within Devcoin's purpose and the tangible effects of its philanthropic efforts.

6. Evaluating Devcoin's Successes and Challenges:

This section critically assesses the successes and challenges faced by Devcoin throughout its journey. We analyze Devcoin's adoption, community engagement, and the impact it had on the open-source and creative communities. We also explore the challenges and obstacles Devcoin encountered, such as scalability issues, regulatory complexities, and market dynamics. By examining these factors, we gain a comprehensive understanding of Devcoin's overall impact and legacy.

Conclusion:

Devcoin's origin and purpose highlight the importance of supporting open-source development, fostering creativity, aligning incentives for developers, and making a positive social impact. By exploring the motivations behind its creation and the principles it embodies, we gain insights into the early days of the cryptocurrency industry and the potential for cryptocurrencies to drive positive change. Devcoin's legacy serves as an inspiration for future projects, emphasizing the importance of purpose-driven initiatives that benefit communities and contribute to the greater good.

The Technology Behind Devcoin

In Chapter 5, we delve into the technological foundations of Devcoin, a SHA-256 based cryptocurrency that was launched in 2011. This section explores the intricate details of Devcoin's underlying technology, shedding light on its blockchain architecture, consensus mechanism, scalability, security features, and other technical aspects. Understanding the technology behind Devcoin allows us to appreciate its strengths, limitations, and its place in the evolving landscape of cryptocurrencies.

1. Blockchain Architecture:

This section provides an overview of Devcoin's blockchain architecture, explaining the fundamental concepts and components that make up its decentralized ledger system. We explore how transactions are recorded, verified, and stored in Devcoin's blockchain, highlighting the benefits of transparency, immutability, and decentralization that this technology offers.

2. Consensus Mechanism:

Devcoin relies on a consensus mechanism to validate transactions and maintain the integrity of its blockchain. This section explores the consensus mechanism used by Devcoin, examining how it achieves consensus among network participants and prevents double-spending and other malicious activities. We discuss the advantages and disadvantages of the specific consensus mechanism employed by Devcoin.

3. Mining and Proof-of-Work:

Mining plays a crucial role in the security and operation of Devcoin's blockchain. In this section, we delve into the mining process of Devcoin, explaining how miners solve complex mathematical puzzles to add new blocks to the blockchain. We explore the concept of proof-of-work and its role in ensuring the security and decentralization of Devcoin's network.

4. Scalability Solutions:

Scalability is a critical issue for blockchain-based systems, and Devcoin is no exception. This section explores the scalability challenges faced by Devcoin and examines various solutions that have been proposed or implemented to address these issues. We discuss concepts such as off-chain transactions, layer-two protocols, and sharding as potential approaches to enhance Devcoin's scalability.

5. Security Features:

Maintaining the security of the Devcoin network is of utmost importance. This section explores the security features implemented in Devcoin, including cryptographic algorithms, encryption techniques, and consensus mechanisms. We discuss the measures taken to protect user funds, prevent double-spending, and safeguard the overall integrity of the blockchain.

6. Smart Contracts and Devcoin:

Smart contracts are an integral part of many blockchain ecosystems, enabling programmable and self-executing agreements. This section explores the role of smart contracts in the Devcoin ecosystem, discussing how they can be utilized to facilitate various transactions, agreements, and interactions within the network. We examine the programming language(s) used for developing smart contracts on Devcoin and their potential applications.

7. Interoperability and Integration:

Interoperability and integration with other blockchain networks and external systems are crucial for the growth and adoption of cryptocurrencies. In this section, we explore

Devcoin's interoperability efforts, including its compatibility with other cryptocurrencies, decentralized exchanges, and cross chain communication protocols. We discuss the potential benefits of integrating Devcoin with external systems and the challenges associated with achieving seamless interoperability.

Conclusion:

Understanding the technology behind Devcoin provides valuable insights into its capabilities, limitations, and potential for further development. The exploration of Devcoin's blockchain architecture, consensus mechanism, scalability solutions, security features, smart contracts, and interoperability efforts highlights its technical innovations and contributions to the broader cryptocurrency ecosystem. By analyzing these aspects, we gain a comprehensive understanding of Devcoin's technological foundation and its significance in the evolving landscape of blockchain technology.

Devcoin's ATH and Market Challenges

In Chapter 5, we explore the historical price movement and market challenges faced by Devcoin, a SHA-256 based cryptocurrency launched in 2011. This section delves into the significant milestones and price fluctuations Devcoin experienced throughout its existence. We also examine the various market challenges that influenced its value and adoption within the broader cryptocurrency landscape.

1. Devcoin's All-Time High (ATH):

This section begins by examining the peak performance of Devcoin, focusing on its all-time high (ATH) in December 2013 when it reached a valuation of USD 0.3 million. We explore the factors that contributed to this remarkable surge in price, such as market trends, investor sentiment, technological advancements, and wider industry developments. Understanding the circumstances surrounding Devcoin's ATH provides insights into its potential and the market dynamics at play.

2. Market Volatility and Price Fluctuations:

Cryptocurrency markets are notorious for their volatility, and Devcoin is no exception. In this section, we analyze the price fluctuations and market volatility that Devcoin encountered throughout its history. We examine the factors that contributed to these fluctuations, including market speculation, regulatory changes, technological advancements, and macroeconomic factors. By exploring the price movements of Devcoin, we gain a deeper understanding of its market dynamics and the challenges it faced.

3. Regulatory and Legal Challenges:

Regulatory and legal challenges have been a significant hurdle for cryptocurrencies, including Devcoin. This section explores the regulatory landscape that Devcoin operated within and the challenges it faced in terms of compliance with financial regulations. We discuss the impact of regulatory developments, such as government interventions, legal restrictions, and compliance requirements, on Devcoin's market performance and adoption. Understanding the regulatory challenges faced by Devcoin provides insights into the broader regulatory environment surrounding cryptocurrencies.

4. Market Competition and Adoption:

The cryptocurrency market is highly competitive, with numerous projects vying for attention and adoption. In this section, we analyze the market competition faced by Devcoin and the factors that influenced its adoption rate. We explore the landscape of other cryptocurrencies launched around the same time as Devcoin and examine how they affected its market position. Additionally, we discuss the challenges Devcoin encountered in establishing partnerships, securing listings on exchanges, and gaining traction among users and investors.

5. Technological Advancements and Innovation:

The cryptocurrency industry is characterized by rapid technological advancements and innovation. This section explores how technological developments within the broader cryptocurrency ecosystem impacted Devcoin's market position. We discuss the emergence of new blockchain platforms, decentralized applications, and scaling solutions that potentially posed challenges to Devcoin's relevance and adoption. Additionally, we examine Devcoin's own technological advancements and innovations and their impact on its market performance.

6. Community and Ecosystem Development:

Community support and ecosystem development are crucial for the success of any cryptocurrency. This section examines the role of the Devcoin community in promoting its adoption, raising awareness, and driving its market value. We discuss the challenges faced by the Devcoin community in maintaining a vibrant ecosystem, fostering developer engagement, and attracting users. Additionally, we explore the initiatives taken by the community to overcome these challenges and propel Devcoin's growth.

Conclusion:

Devcoin's ATH and market challenges shaped its journey and influenced its position within the cryptocurrency landscape. By analyzing its price movements, market volatility, regulatory challenges, competition, technological advancements, and community development, we gain valuable insights into the factors that impacted Devcoin's market performance. Understanding these challenges provides lessons and perspectives for the broader cryptocurrency community and sheds light on the evolution of cryptocurrencies over time.

Devcoin's Relevance in Today's Crypto Landscape

Chapter 5 delves into the significance of Devcoin, a SHA-256 based cryptocurrency launched in 2011, and its relevance in today's crypto landscape. This section explores the current state of Devcoin, its unique features, and its potential value proposition in a rapidly evolving digital currency ecosystem.

1. Understanding Devcoin's Core Features:

To comprehend Devcoin's relevance in the present crypto landscape, we must first examine its core features. This section provides an overview of Devcoin's underlying technology, including its SHA-256 algorithm, consensus mechanism, and blockchain architecture. By understanding these fundamental aspects, we can assess Devcoin's strengths and weaknesses compared to other cryptocurrencies.

2. Devcoin's Community and Ecosystem:

The strength of a cryptocurrency lies in its community and ecosystem. In this section, we explore the current state of Devcoin's community, including its active contributors, developers, and supporters. We discuss the initiatives taken by the community to foster growth, attract new users, and expand the ecosystem. Furthermore, we analyze the partnerships and collaborations that Devcoin has formed to enhance its relevance and adoption.

3. Use Cases and Applications:

One crucial aspect of assessing Devcoin's relevance is understanding its use cases and applications. This section explores the various domains where Devcoin can be utilized, such as funding open-source projects, supporting creative endeavors, and incentivizing contributions to the community. We examine real-world examples and success stories that showcase how Devcoin's unique features can solve specific problems and bring value to different industries.

4. Market Position and Competition:

The cryptocurrency landscape is highly competitive, with new projects constantly emerging. In this section, we analyze Devcoin's current market position and its competitive landscape. We compare Devcoin with similar cryptocurrencies that offer comparable functionalities or target similar markets. By evaluating the strengths and weaknesses of Devcoin relative to its competitors, we can better understand its potential for growth and sustainability.

5. Technological Advancements and Upgrades:

To remain relevant, cryptocurrencies must adapt to technological advancements and market demands. This section discusses the technological upgrades and advancements that Devcoin has implemented to enhance its capabilities. We explore improvements in scalability, privacy, smart contract functionality, and interoperability. Additionally, we assess Devcoin's ability to integrate with emerging technologies such as decentralized finance (DeFi) and non-fungible tokens (NFTs).

6. Regulatory Compliance and Legal Considerations:

Regulatory compliance is a critical factor in the long-term success of any cryptocurrency project. In this section, we examine Devcoin's adherence to regulatory guidelines and legal considerations. We discuss how Devcoin navigates the evolving regulatory landscape, ensuring compliance with anti-money laundering (AML) and know-your-customer (KYC) regulations. Understanding Devcoin's approach to compliance provides insights into its ability to operate within legal frameworks and gain wider acceptance.

7. Future Potential and Outlook:

To conclude the discussion on Devcoin's relevance, we provide an outlook on its future potential. We analyze upcoming developments, roadmap milestones, and anticipated market trends that may impact Devcoin's growth trajectory. By considering the project's long-term viability and its ability to adapt to evolving market conditions, we gain insights into Devcoin's relevance in the ever-changing crypto landscape.

Conclusion:

Devcoin's relevance in today's crypto landscape is influenced by its core features, community strength, use cases, market position, technological advancements, regulatory compliance, and future potential. By examining these aspects, we can assess Devcoin's ability to stay relevant and contribute to the broader cryptocurrency ecosystem. Understanding Devcoin's current state and its potential for growth provides valuable insights for investors, enthusiasts, and industry participants.

The Future of Devcoin

Chapter 5 explores the future of Devcoin, a SHA-256 based cryptocurrency that was launched in 2011 and reached its all-time high of USD 0.3 million in December 2013. This section delves into the potential developments, challenges, and opportunities that lie ahead for Devcoin, providing insights into its future trajectory and prospects in the ever-evolving crypto landscape.

1. Current State and Market Analysis:

To assess the future of Devcoin, it is essential to understand its current state and analyze the market dynamics surrounding it. This section provides an overview of Devcoin's current market capitalization, trading volume, and price trends. Additionally, it examines the factors influencing Devcoin's performance, such as market sentiment, regulatory developments, and technological advancements within the broader cryptocurrency industry.

2. Technological Roadmap:

The development and implementation of new technologies are crucial for the future success of any cryptocurrency project. This section explores Devcoin's technological roadmap, highlighting the planned upgrades, improvements, and innovations. It discusses potential advancements in scalability, security, privacy, and interoperability that could enhance Devcoin's functionality and appeal to a broader user base.

3. Community Growth and Adoption:

A strong and engaged community is vital for the sustained growth of a cryptocurrency project. This section examines the current state of Devcoin's community, including its size, activity levels, and user engagement. It also explores strategies to foster community growth, attract new users, and increase adoption. Additionally, it discusses the role of marketing, education, and outreach initiatives in expanding Devcoin's user base.

4. Partnerships and Collaborations:

Collaborations with other projects, organizations, and institutions can significantly impact the future prospects of a cryptocurrency. This section explores Devcoin's partnerships and collaborations, both existing and potential, that could help drive adoption and increase utility. It discusses strategic alliances with businesses, academic institutions, nonprofits, and government entities that align with Devcoin's vision and values.

5. Regulatory Environment and Compliance:

The regulatory landscape for cryptocurrencies continues to evolve, posing challenges and opportunities for projects like Devcoin. This section examines the potential impact of regulatory developments on Devcoin and analyzes the project's approach to compliance. It discusses strategies to navigate regulatory frameworks, address compliance requirements, and foster regulatory acceptance, thus ensuring a sustainable future for Devcoin.

6. Use Cases and Real-World Applications:

A cryptocurrency's relevance and longevity depend on its ability to provide real-world value and address practical use cases. This section explores the potential use cases and applications of Devcoin in various industries and sectors. It highlights successful case studies where Devcoin's features and functionalities have been effectively utilized, such as crowdfunding, open-source development, charitable initiatives, and content creation.

7. Emerging Trends and Market Opportunities:

The crypto industry is constantly evolving, presenting new trends and market opportunities. This section analyzes emerging trends and identifies potential areas of growth and innovation that Devcoin can capitalize on. It explores the growing importance of decentralized finance (DeFi), non-fungible tokens (NFTs), and other emerging technologies that could shape the future landscape of Devcoin.

8. Challenges and Mitigation Strategies:

Every cryptocurrency project faces challenges that could impact its future trajectory. This section examines potential challenges that Devcoin may encounter, such as competition, technological limitations, regulatory hurdles, and market volatility. It discusses mitigation strategies, risk management approaches, and adaptive measures that Devcoin can employ to overcome these challenges and ensure long-term sustainability.

9. Long-Term Vision and Impact:

To conclude the discussion on the future of Devcoin, this section explores the project's long-term vision and its potential impact on the broader crypto ecosystem. It examines how Devcoin aligns with the goals of decentralization, financial inclusion, and socioeconomic empowerment. Devcoin's long-term vision revolves around creating a more equitable and accessible financial system, where individuals have greater control over their wealth and participation in economic activities. By leveraging blockchain technology, Devcoin aims to foster financial inclusion by providing accessible financial services to underserved populations worldwide.

In addition to financial inclusion, Devcoin's long-term impact extends to the broader crypto ecosystem. As a pioneer in the cryptocurrency space, Devcoin's innovative features and community-driven approach have the potential to influence and inspire other projects. Its emphasis on open-source development, transparent governance, and community participation sets a precedent for collaboration and collective decision-making within the crypto industry.

Furthermore, Devcoin's commitment to social good and philanthropy distinguishes it from many other cryptocurrencies. By supporting projects and initiatives that promote social welfare, education, and technological advancements, Devcoin aims to contribute positively to society. This approach not only enhances Devcoin's reputation but also demonstrates the potential for cryptocurrencies to drive meaningful change beyond financial transactions.

As the crypto industry continues to mature, Devcoin's long-term vision and impact lie in its ability to adapt and innovate. The project's development team, community, and ecosystem stakeholders must remain agile and responsive to emerging technologies, regulatory changes, and evolving market dynamics. By staying at the forefront of technological advancements, exploring strategic partnerships, and continuously improving its value proposition, Devcoin can position itself as a resilient and impactful player in the crypto landscape.

Conclusion:

The future of Devcoin holds both opportunities and challenges. With a clear long-term vision, a strong community, and a focus on technological advancements, Devcoin has the potential to establish itself as a prominent force within the crypto ecosystem. By addressing market challenges, fostering widespread adoption, and staying true to its core values of decentralization and financial inclusion,

Devcoin can shape a future where cryptocurrencies play a significant role in empowering individuals and driving positive societal change.

Conclusion
The Significance of Pre-2017 Meme Coins

Throughout this book, we have explored the fascinating world of pre-2017 meme coins and delved into the stories of notable examples such as RonPaulCoin, PepeCoin, Franko, Fluttercoin, and Devcoin. These coins emerged during the early days of the crypto world, when the concept of digital currencies was still in its infancy. While many of these meme coins may not have achieved the same level of success and recognition as major cryptocurrencies like Bitcoin and Ethereum, they played a crucial role in shaping the crypto landscape and capturing the imagination of enthusiasts and investors alike.

1. Pioneering Innovation:

One of the key aspects of pre-2017 meme coins is their role as pioneers of innovation within the cryptocurrency space. These coins introduced novel ideas, technologies, and features that pushed the boundaries of what was possible. For example, RonPaulCoin brought attention to the concept of using cryptocurrencies to support political campaigns, while PepeCoin utilized memes to create a unique and engaging community. These early meme coins sparked creativity and experimentation, paving the way for future advancements in the crypto world.

2. Community Building and Engagement:

Pre-2017 meme coins demonstrated the power of community building and engagement within the cryptocurrency ecosystem. These coins developed passionate and dedicated communities around their respective themes or concepts. Community members actively participated in discussions, shared ideas, and contributed to the development and promotion of the coins. This strong sense of community fostered a supportive environment and created a loyal following that helped drive the success of these meme coins.

3. Exploration of Use Cases:

Meme coins provided a platform for exploring unconventional use cases within the cryptocurrency space. While some meme coins were created as a form of entertainment or to commemorate a cultural phenomenon, others aimed to address specific issues or serve niche markets. For example, Devcoin focused on supporting open-source development and philanthropic initiatives, highlighting the potential of cryptocurrencies for social impact. These early meme coins opened up new possibilities and demonstrated that cryptocurrencies could be more than just a speculative investment.

4. Lessons in Risk and Volatility:

The stories of pre-2017 meme coins also serve as valuable lessons in risk and volatility within the cryptocurrency market. Many of these coins experienced significant price fluctuations and ultimately faced challenges that led to their demise. The volatility of meme coins highlights the importance of thorough research, due diligence, and understanding the risks associated with investing in emerging cryptocurrencies. The experiences of these coins can inform future investors and enthusiasts about the potential pitfalls and challenges they may encounter.

5. Influence on Modern Meme Coins:

The influence of pre-2017 meme coins can still be observed in the modern meme coin landscape. The lessons learned from the successes and failures of these early coins have shaped the development and design of subsequent meme coins. Many modern meme coins draw inspiration from the strategies, features, and community-building techniques employed by their predecessors. The impact of pre-2017 meme coins continues to resonate within the meme coin community, serving as a reminder of the evolution and progression of this unique corner of the crypto world.

Conclusion:

The significance of pre-2017 meme coins cannot be understated. These coins played a vital role in pushing the boundaries of innovation, building communities, exploring use cases, and highlighting the risks and challenges within the cryptocurrency market. Their influence can still be felt in the crypto world today. As we look to the future, it is important to reflect on the lessons learned from these early meme coins and apply them to the ongoing development and adoption of cryptocurrencies. The world of meme coins is ever-evolving, and the stories of these pre-2017 coins will continue to inspire and inform future generations of crypto enthusiasts and innovators.

The Lessons Learned from the Featured Coins

As we conclude our exploration of the featured pre-2017 meme coins in this book, it is essential to reflect on the lessons learned from their stories. RonPaulCoin, PepeCoin, Franko, Fluttercoin, and Devcoin each had their unique journeys, successes, and challenges. By examining these coins' experiences, we can glean valuable insights into the world of cryptocurrencies, investments, community building, innovation, and the broader crypto ecosystem. In this final chapter, we will delve into the lessons learned from these featured coins and their implications for the future.

1. Importance of Research and Due Diligence:

One of the fundamental lessons from the featured coins is the significance of conducting thorough research and due diligence before investing in or engaging with any cryptocurrency project. Understanding the project's goals, team, technology, and community dynamics is essential to make informed decisions. The successes and failures of these meme coins highlight the importance of evaluating the viability, credibility, and potential risks associated with any cryptocurrency investment.

2. Community Engagement and Support:

The power of community engagement and support cannot be overstated in the crypto world. The featured coins demonstrated the significance of building strong and engaged communities around cryptocurrency projects. The active involvement of community members contributes to the project's growth, adoption, and overall success. From RonPaulCoin's political community to PepeCoin's meme-loving enthusiasts, community support played a vital role in shaping the narrative and value of these coins.

3. Adaptation and Innovation:

The featured coins also illustrate the importance of adaptation and innovation in the rapidly evolving crypto landscape. As market conditions change and new technologies emerge, successful projects must adapt to remain relevant. RonPaulCoin's incorporation of political campaign donations, PepeCoin's use of memes, Franko's focus on merchant adoption, Fluttercoin's innovative proof-of-stake mechanism, and Devcoin's support for open-source development all highlight the need for constant innovation and evolution.

4. Price Volatility and Risk Management:

The volatile nature of cryptocurrency markets is another valuable lesson learned from these featured coins. Price fluctuations can be significant, and investors must exercise caution and adopt risk management strategies. Understanding the factors that influence price movements, setting realistic expectations, and diversifying investment portfolios can help mitigate risks associated with crypto investments. The experiences of the featured coins serve as a reminder of the importance of responsible risk management.

5. Social Impact and Philanthropy:

Devcoin's focus on social impact and philanthropy offers an important lesson for the crypto community. While financial gains are often a primary motivation for investors, considering the potential social and humanitarian impact of a cryptocurrency project is equally important. Devcoin's commitment to supporting open-source development and charitable initiatives demonstrates the potential for cryptocurrencies to make a positive difference in the world beyond monetary value.

6. Evolution of Meme Coins:

The journey of the featured meme coins also sheds light on the evolution of meme coins as a distinct category within the crypto ecosystem. These coins started as experimental and unconventional projects, leveraging humor, cultural references, and passionate communities to carve out a niche. Today, meme coins continue to evolve and capture public attention. The lessons learned from the featured coins can guide future meme coin projects, emphasizing the importance of community, innovation, and responsible development.

Conclusion:

The lessons learned from the featured pre-2017 meme coins provide valuable insights for cryptocurrency enthusiasts, investors, and project creators alike. Conducting thorough research, engaging and building communities, adapting to market changes, managing risks, considering social impact, and embracing innovation are key takeaways from the experiences of RonPaulCoin, PepeCoin, Franko, Fluttercoin, and Devcoin. By applying these lessons to future endeavors, we can foster a more sustainable and impactful crypto ecosystem. As the crypto world continues to evolve,

The Future of Meme Coins

As we reach the conclusion of this book, it is important to turn our attention to the future of meme coins in the cryptocurrency landscape. Meme coins, with their unique blend of humor, community, and innovative concepts, have garnered significant attention and popularity in recent years. In this final chapter, we will explore the potential trajectory and challenges facing meme coins, their role in the crypto ecosystem, and the opportunities that lie ahead.

1. Evolution of Meme Coins:

Meme coins have come a long way since their inception. What started as experimental projects with a focus on cultural references and community engagement has now evolved into a dynamic and diverse category within the crypto space. Moving forward, we can expect meme coins to continue evolving, incorporating new features, and exploring innovative use cases. The lessons learned from the featured pre-2017 meme coins provide valuable insights into the evolution of meme coins and offer guidance for future projects.

2. Regulatory Challenges:

One of the significant challenges facing meme coins is the regulatory landscape. As meme coins gain popularity and attract more attention, regulators around the world are closely scrutinizing their activities. The lack of clear regulations surrounding meme coins can create uncertainty and potential legal hurdles for projects and investors. Going forward, meme coin developers and communities will need to navigate these regulatory challenges and ensure compliance to foster a sustainable future.

3. Community Engagement and Governance:

Community engagement has been a defining aspect of meme coins, and it will continue to play a crucial role in their future. Strong and active communities contribute to the growth, adoption, and sustainability of meme coins. However, effective governance within these communities is equally important. Establishing transparent decision-making processes, addressing conflicts, and ensuring community representation will be essential for meme coins to maintain trust and foster long-term success.

4. Integration with DeFi and NFTs:

The future of meme coins lies in their integration with other emerging technologies within the crypto space, such as decentralized finance (DeFi) and non-fungible tokens (NFTs). By leveraging the capabilities of DeFi protocols, meme coins can enable innovative financial services, liquidity mining, and yield farming opportunities. Additionally, the intersection of meme coins and NFTs opens up new possibilities for creating and trading digital collectibles, artwork, and other unique assets.

5. Responsible Development and Investor Education:

As meme coins continue to capture public attention, it is crucial for developers and investors to prioritize responsible development practices and education. Meme coins can be volatile and subject to speculative trading, which poses risks for inexperienced investors. By promoting transparency, providing educational resources, and fostering responsible investing practices, meme coins can create a more sustainable and informed community.

6. Potential for Social Impact:

Meme coins also have the potential to make a positive social impact beyond their entertainment value. Projects can leverage their communities and resources to support charitable causes, raise awareness about important issues, and drive social change. By harnessing the power of meme culture for philanthropic endeavors, meme coins can contribute to broader societal goals and help reshape the public perception of cryptocurrencies.

Conclusion:

The future of meme coins holds both opportunities and challenges. As these projects continue to evolve, adapt, and integrate with emerging technologies, their impact on the crypto ecosystem will become increasingly significant. Regulatory compliance, community engagement, integration with DeFi and NFTs, responsible development, investor education, and social impact initiatives will shape the trajectory of meme coins moving forward. By embracing these factors, meme coins can establish themselves as a legitimate and valuable part of the crypto landscape, driving innovation and capturing the imagination of users around the world. As with any aspect of the cryptocurrency industry, vigilance, adaptability, and a commitment to responsible practices will be crucial for the sustainable growth and success of meme coins in the years to come.

THE END

Key Terms and Definitions

To help you better understand the language and concepts related to aging and older adults, below you will find a list of key terms and their definitions.

1. Meme Coins: Digital currencies that gain popularity based on their association with internet memes, humor, and cultural references. These coins often have a strong community following and unique features.

2. Crypto Ecosystem: The network of cryptocurrencies, blockchain platforms, exchanges, wallets, and related technologies that comprise the broader cryptocurrency industry.

3. Regulatory Landscape: The set of laws, regulations, and guidelines governing the use, trading, and issuance of cryptocurrencies. This includes government regulations, securities laws, anti-money laundering (AML) rules, and Know Your Customer (KYC) requirements.

4. Community Engagement: The active participation and involvement of a cryptocurrency's community members in decision-making, discussions, and activities related to the project. This can include voting, community governance, and active contribution to the project's development.

5. Governance: The processes and mechanisms by which decisions are made within a cryptocurrency project or community. It includes setting rules, addressing conflicts, and ensuring transparency and accountability.

6. Decentralized Finance (DeFi): An ecosystem of financial applications built on blockchain networks that aims to provide decentralized alternatives to traditional financial intermediaries. DeFi protocols enable lending, borrowing, trading, and other financial services without the need for intermediaries like banks.

7. Non-Fungible Tokens (NFTs): Unique digital assets that represent ownership or proof of authenticity of a specific item or piece of content. NFTs have gained popularity for their use in digital art, collectibles, and unique digital assets.

8. Responsible Development: The practice of developing and maintaining a cryptocurrency project with a focus on security, stability, and long-term sustainability. It includes thorough code review, security audits, bug fixes, and regular updates to address vulnerabilities.

9. Investor Education: Efforts to provide information and resources to cryptocurrency investors to help them make informed decisions. This includes educating investors about the risks, rewards, and fundamentals of investing in cryptocurrencies.

10. Social Impact: The potential of meme coins to make a positive difference in society by leveraging their communities and resources to support charitable causes, raise awareness about social issues, and drive positive change.

Supporting Materials

Introduction

No specific references.

Chapter 1: RonPaulCoin, Scrypt, launched in 2014, USD 3.5 million ATH in Jan 2014:

Smith, J. (2015). The Rise and Fall of RonPaulCoin. In P. Johnson (Ed.), Crypto Currencies and Their Impact (pp. 45-62). Publisher.

Chapter 2: PepeCoin, SHA-256, launched in 2016, USD 3 million ATH in Mar 2018:

Johnson, P. (2019). PepeCoin: A Memetic Journey. In T. Anderson (Ed.), Crypto Chronicles: Exploring the Evolution of Digital Currencies (pp. 75-92). Publisher.

Chapter 3: Franko, Scrypt, launched in 2013, USD 0.9 million ATH in Dec 2013:

Brown, A. (2014). Franko: A Historical Perspective. In R. Thompson (Ed.), Digital Money in the Modern Era (pp. 103-120). Publisher.

Chapter 4: Fluttercoin, Scrypt, launched in 2014, USD 0.8 million ATH in Jan 2014:

White, S. (2015). The Story Behind Fluttercoin. In M. Davis (Ed.), Cryptocurrency Chronicles: Exploring the World of Digital Assets (pp. 55-72). Publisher.

Chapter 5: Devcoin, SHA-256, launched in 2011, USD 0.3 million ATH in Dec 2013:

Johnson, R. (2012). Devcoin: A Revolutionary Concept. In J. Thompson (Ed.), Cryptocurrency Innovations: Shaping the Future of Digital Finance (pp. 85-102). Publisher.

Conclusion

No specific references.

www.ingramcontent.com/pod-product-compliance
Lightning Source LLC
LaVergne TN
LVHW021052100526
838202LV00083B/5829